THE FREE MAN AND THE SOLDIER

THE FREE MAN AND THE SOLDIER

ESSAYS ON THE RECONCILIATION OF LIBERTY AND DISCIPLINE

BY

RALPH BARTON PERRY

BOOKS FOR LIBRARIES PRESS
FREEPORT, NEW YORK

First Published 1916

Reprinted 1970

STANDARD BOOK NUMBER:
8369-5438-6

LIBRARY OF CONGRESS CATALOG CARD NUMBER:
73-124250

PRINTED IN THE UNITED STATES OF AMERICA

AFFECTIONATELY DEDICATED

TO

S. B. P.

PREFACE

THE sort of truth that is in most danger of getting itself ignored is the whole truth. It is usually too monotonously obvious to attract attention, too insipid to lend a relish to conversation, and too dull to point a paragraph. Half-truths hold the stage, and divide the allegiance of mankind among them. Thus, instead of agreeing that we are somewhere in the middle of progress, with something done and something yet to do, opinion is divided between the old and the young, between those who believe that the world is rapidly approaching its end and those who believe that it has just begun. Optimist and pessimist, anarchist and reactionary, atheist and bigot, feminist and misogynist, these are some of the character-parts which the human mind admires and loves to assume. The present crisis in human affairs has given a fearful urgency to two great human problems. First, how shall one be secure and yet peaceful? Second, how shall we act in concert and yet remain free individuals? In each case the solution of the problem requires the reconciliation of two indispensable values. And yet men divide themselves into parties and become blind to one of these values through excess of zeal for the other. Thus militarists for security's sake abandon the ideal of peace, and pacifists for the sake of peace shut their eyes to violence and danger. Or individualists in the name of freedom protest against organization and authority; while nationalists from love of country forget that no country is worthy of being loved that is not the home of independent and happy individuals. Thus the solid truth escapes notice, from too much looking at one or another of its flat surfaces. Even if the truth be hard to win, it is worth something to see it on both sides and to comprehend its dimensions. Whatever be sound policy in the present crisis it must provide a way by which liberty and peace shall be consistent with solidarity and strength; by which a man may take his place as a soldier in the ranks, and yet remain free.

Essays I, II, IV, and V have appeared in part in *The New Republic ;* VI and XI in *The Atlantic Monthly ;* VII in *The International Journal of*

Ethics ; VIII in *The New York Times ;* X in *The Forum ;* and XII in *Harper's Weekly.* My thanks are due to the editors of these periodicals for permission to reprint.

RALPH BARTON PERRY.

CAMBRIDGE, MASS., June 15, 1916.

CONTENTS

THE FREE MAN AND THE SOLDIER

I

THE FREE MAN AND THE SOLDIER

WHEN General Miles on a recent occasion expressed himself as opposed to universal military service, he was quoted as saying that the American people would never allow themselves to be "Prussianized." It is customary to say that if a people is to be trained to arms they must become spiritually or fundamentally "regimented." This dictum has usually passed unchallenged. It is regarded as a sort of axiom, which even the extremest advocates of preparedness are rarely bold enough to deny. And yet curiously enough, even the superficial facts are against it. Thus, whatever we mean by that individualism which we prize, we do not look to China for examples of it. China, whether justly or unjustly, signifies to Occidental minds that very uniformity and stagnation which points the moral, and yet China is notable among the nations for its lack of military discipline. France, on the other hand, was for centuries the most soldierly nation of Europe, and has in recent years made the most exacting military demands upon her citizens. Yet France remains pre-eminently liberal and cosmopolitan. France is a perpetual source of novelty, of modernisms and futurisms, of those departures from tradition and type, those excesses and daring conceits which scandalize and inspire, and which spring from a free mind roaming at large in its world.

What shall we say of ourselves? We have been let alone for half a century. No drill-master has taught us to keep alignments and intervals or to step a regulation thirty inches. No bugle-call has intruded upon our private affairs and summoned us to march the same road. We have not been swept by collective passion or articulated in any smooth-working mechanism. But what have we been doing? Have we become individuals? Are we eminent among the nations as a race of ample personalities? Are our laboring men notable for self-respect and self-sufficiency? Does our leisured class breed creative genius, or our political life leadership and constructive statesmanship? What, then, is this individualism which we are so afraid to lose?

Let us be willing to say of ourselves what we would not unnaturally resent if it were uttered by an alien critic. We are a bit sodden, a bit too fond of what money will buy. We are not guiltless of hiring an army in order to enjoy our Carthaginian ease. We enjoy irresponsibility as the child enjoys it. Some few, having a day full of "engagements" and pastimes, would like to be left uninterrupted. The great majority are solaced by the hope of rising in life to the same privilege or are embittered by their exclusion from it. The absence of discipline has not, then, perfected us as individuals, though it may have tolerated our selfishness and spread wide the envious hope of making a fortune. Indeed, the absence of a more conscious and rational collectivism has rendered us peculiarly defenseless against factional solidarities, against vogues and fads, against contagious sentimentalities and unscrupulous demagoguery. We are notoriously afraid of the mass opinion that we help to create. We have the greatest respect for the normal, and are quick to catch and echo the popular note. There are so many ears to the ground that there is often nothing to hear except the confused noise created by so much listening.

When we turn to our political liberties, on the other hand, we can speak with greater confidence. Liberty of the press, trial by jury, freedom of speech, popular government, self-respecting civic autonomy, these are solid goods. These we justly believe to be spiritual achievements, by which we would like history to know us. But these are collective achievements, founded in organization and secured by organization. We do not owe them to our laxity and incohesiveness, but to constitutions and to laws. They exist not by virtue of private self-assertion, but by virtue of a disciplined regard for the rights of others. We owe them to that tradition and experience which impels us with loyal accord to support a system that defines our mutual relations and establishes our collective life.

If we cannot point to ourselves as bright examples of the blessings of undisciplined freedom, there remains, perhaps, the example of England, or the contrast of England and Germany. The war has already proved the necessity, for specifically military purposes, of national organization and universal service. If the Allies win the war it will be because having tardily acquired these virtues they enjoy certain residual advantages as well. But while this is granted, it will be said that England has owed her superior individualism to her lack of just such military organization and discipline, and that Germany has sacrificed individualism in order to possess them. Now I am one of those who believe that England does possess an individualism which Germany lacks, and that this individualism is a mark of superiority. Even this is not unqualifiedly true in view of the degree of snobbery and class antagonism which mars the democracy of England. But the fact remains that England is pre-eminently the home of men who know their rights and who sturdily insist upon them. Through combining independence with steadiness and practical sagacity, England has forged our constitutional liberties, has disseminated the spirit of tolerance and self-criticism, and has insisted upon owning and using her institutions instead of being enslaved or absorbed by them. In Germany, on the other hand, there is a certain political flabbiness, which tolerates authority too easily. Even art, science, and religion, which ought to emancipate the individual, have become a means of confirming and sanctifying his submission.

If this be the case, it is nevertheless important to avoid confusing causes and effects, or assuming without reason that things which happen together are therefore causally and inseparably related. The Englishman's opposition to universal military service is undoubtedly associated in his own mind with the individualism he admires and claims as his own. But the opposition is not, I think, so much a logical defense of his individualism as a temperamental expression of it, a sort of psychological by-product. He would prefer to serve his country in war just as he would prefer to do anything else, as a matter of "sport," or from the motive of noblesse oblige, or out of fondness for tradition. He doesn't like anything that looks too orderly and prescribed, too freshly and deliberately made. He is fond of his crotchets, and regards reason as a sort of parvenu. Trollope wrote of one of his more doubtful characters: "He isn't of our sort. He's too clever, too cosmopolitan—a sort of man whitewashed of all prejudices, who wouldn't mind whether he ate horseflesh or beef if horseflesh were as good as beef, and never had an association in his life." Universal military training is too rational, too schematic, too exclusively mindful of the bare utilities and essentials. The Englishman shrinks from it as he shrinks from an adequate national system of education, or from the metric system, or from phonetic spelling. If it could only become a tradition like royalty and the top-hat, or an adventure like governing India and playing football, or a matter of instinct like the morning tub, he would cling to it until it had long since become obsolete. For the military virtues in themselves are unobjectionable. It is not the substance of the thing, but rather the deliberate act of adoption that is repugnant to English individualism. It is impossible to believe that once in vogue such a system would in the least abridge an Englishman's essential liberties or seriously alter the peculiar tone of his national life.

That it is the methodical rather than the compulsory element in a universal system of training and service which has stood in the way of its acceptance in England, appears in the readiness with which the pressure of public opinion is used as a means of coercion. The voluntary theory implies that men *shall* volunteer. It does not mean that men shall freely choose to serve or not to serve, according to taste or aptitude, but that they shall choose *service* according as national exigencies shall dictate. In practise this leads inevitably to the ugliest sort of coercion. Many men who nominally volunteer are as a matter of fact shamed into it. They are shamed into it at first by example. If that does not suffice they are called hard names, such as "slackers." Unorganized pressure gives place in time to organized pressure. Among those who are thus systematically persecuted are many who not unnaturally resent an interference with what they have been taught to believe is their just liberty of action. The remnant thus harried and cornered is eventually coerced by conscription; which when thus arrived at, as a measure of last resort, is unblushing tyranny. The whole process, in short, is one of first conferring rights and then outraging them by sheer force. Where, on the other hand, the state is legally entitled to the military service of its citizens, as it is entitled to some fraction of their property, military service is taken for granted. It is acknowledged as an obligation, and is sustained by the law-abiding habits of the community. It is accepted in the spirit of fair play, as part of that general order of life which a free man accepts as a contracting beneficiary.

Universal military service is otherwise opposed in England for economic reasons of a very different sort. The laboring man not unjustly feels that he is a creditor and not a debtor in his relations to the state. To him compulsory service savors of tyranny because it is imposed upon him by an authority that has neglected him. The tradition of laissez-faire, which has taught him that he must look out for himself, has not taught him to be grateful. In so far as the state absolves itself of responsibility it can impose no obligations. The moral of this difficulty is not that universal military service should therefore be rejected, but that the state should inspire and deserve the loyalty of its citizens through a just regard for their needs. Indeed, we are brought back to a much more fundamental and far-reaching question than any which concerns merely military exigencies alone. Laissez-faire fosters a complacent selfishness among the successful, an aggressive selfishness among the hopeful, an envious selfishness among those who are unsuccessful, and a bitter selfishness among those who are hopeless. If this be individualism, the less of it the better. Neither its spirit nor its fruits are to be numbered among the blessings of English civilization. And in so far as it operates as a cause of opposition to universal military service, it argues for rather than against such a system.

If England affords no evidence that the absence of universal military service is the cause of an individualism that is worthy and admirable, it will yet be argued that Germany illustrates the blighting effects of its adoption. That the military system of Germany forms part of a dynastic, bureaucratic and cultural system which as a whole is prejudicial to the best individualism does not, I think, require proof. One does not look to Germany for a tolerant cosmopolitanism, or for a jealous insistence upon the great civil liberties. But this is not a direct and necessary consequence of its military mechanism. It is due to the purpose which directs that mechanism: to the spirit which dominates it, and the use which is made of it. The deeper causes are to be found in the Prussian traditions of conquest and dynastic right, in the Germanic philosophy of the state as absorbing and superseding its citizens, and perhaps in a racial propensity to domineer. These ideas find in the military system a harsh and effective mode of expression. But the army is the instrument and not the cause. A fraternal and chivalrous people like the French have created a fraternal and chivalrous army. An unaggressive and home-loving people like the Swiss have created a defensive army. A democratic and radical people like the Australians have adapted a national military system to their ideals of popular government and the dignity of labor.

Military preparedness in itself means nothing more than foresight and organization applied to the contingency of war. The alternative is blindness and confusion. War is an actuality and a genuine peril. It is, furthermore, a peril which threatens the *collective* life; there is no interest, however exalted, that is immune. Preparedness is therefore every man's concern. A national system of training and service is simply the responsible, concerted, and effective way of meeting this peril. But the spirit which animates a military organization, on the other hand, will reflect the interests which men desire to safeguard. If we in America desire to be and remain free, if there is a peculiar tone of personal independence and equality that is the breath of life to us, then that is the end to which our military organization will be consecrated, and that is the spirit which we shall carry with us into it. If we are to be free, we must be safely and effectively free. There must be a place secured for freedom, and to secure that freedom, free men may be soldiers.

A deliberate and rational concert of action does not hamper individuality. If there is any one incontrovertible principle that governs life, it is this: that freedom does not come of letting things take their course. Free individuals are not spontaneously generated by the bare removal of restrictions; they are the products of discipline and order. A freedom that knows no bounds is the conceit of impatient and careless minds. A military system that is imposed from without, or hastily improvised in a moment of panic, may indeed be tyrannical. But a system freely adopted, in order to do loyally and skilfully that which must be done, is primarily a matter of morale and character. Over and above that it will vary with the genius and aims of the people who create it and enter into it.

Since war is an actuality and a genuine peril, let us soberly undertake the burden it imposes. Let us cultivate the soldierly qualities, and let us equip ourselves with the tools which are effective in modern warfare. Let us acquire the capacity for organized action, and be ready for the occasion which a rational man will both fear and deprecate. But let us be such soldiers as we would be men. If we are lovers of liberty and devotees of peace, let us inscribe these ideals on our banners.

II

THE VIGIL OF ARMS

IT was thought appropriate that a man should pass the eve of his knighthood "bestowing himself in orisons and prayers." A knight should be a good knight, "a noble and gentle knight"— one dedicated to service and jealous of honor. Power is admirable only when restrained. Physical strength in a man is justified only by the weakness which it succors, by the incorporeal things to which it gives a body. Unless their use is redeemed by necessity or by some humane cause, arms are merely cruel and mischievous. The sentiments and symbols associated with war are ways of recognizing its inherent hatefulness. They are the means of concealing the ugly truth that arms are devised to kill with. If the use of arms can be judged even tolerable it must be because of the soldier's code and the soldier's cause.

Hence a nation about to arm itself should confess its sins and renew allegiance to its ideals. The knight took vows to protect the holy sepulchre, "to maintain and defend all ladies, gentlewomen, orphans, widows, women distressed and abandoned," or to perfect himself in purity, fidelity and honesty. It will not do to substitute for a code so exacting as that of chivalry, or a cause so clear as that of the crusades, a mere indeterminate vow of patriotism. Loyalty to one's country, unless one understands its policy and helps to mould it, is simply a shirking of the prior obligation to think for oneself.

Military service is at once a necessity, a good and a danger. But it is primarily a necessity. By this I mean that it is justified only as a means to an imperative end. It is not to be undertaken for itself, nor is it lightly to be adopted as a means. Nothing short of national safety or some higher design of international justice and order, can make it reasonable to cultivate the art of destruction. But since military service is so justified, as a painful necessity like surgery, capital punishment or self-sacrifice, it is reasonable that it should be done well, and soberly undertaken as a function of the state. In a democracy this means that it should be acknowledged and assumed as an obligation by all citizens. For democracy implies that there shall be neither privilege nor immunity. "All the inhabitants of the state are its defenders by birth," said Scharn-

horst. If this could be said of Prussia, it can be
said with greater reason of a country like our
own which proclaims the principle of civic equality.

The scale and the method of modern warfare
make universal training not only an appropriate
means, but an indispensable means. An untrained
nation depending on a small professional army or
on a horde of "embattled farmers" and other in-
dignant citizens, presents the same pitiful spectacle as that afforded by the dervishes who fought
Kitchener with spears at Omdurman. An armed
man attacked with the naked fist, shot and shell
opposed by bows and arrows, men trained to
use the most improved implements of war resisted by equally brave men who have hith-
erto handled nothing but a hammer, spade,
trowel, tennis-racket, billiard-cue or umbrella—
this is not magnificent, or even absurd; it is
heart-breaking. Those who make it possible by
their stubborn complacency or irrelevant idealism,
are in effect as culpable as those who, because
they preferred the individual to the group, and
counted the soul's culture more important than
mere bodily safety, might consent that undrilled
children should crowd an inflammable school-
house.

The opposition to universal training, like the opposition to more limited forms of preparedness, is due more to ignorance than to principle. Thus our recently appointed Secretary of War confesses that he has changed his ideas as to the sufficiency of our military resources. He is reported to have said that "it is simply a matter of getting information."[1] He has discovered that a slight additional complication on the Mexican border would make it necessary to call upon "the entire standing army of the United States." "One cannot," he adds sagely, "consider such facts as that from an inside angle without realizing that our army would be totally inadequate to handle a real war difficulty!" The naïveté of this confession is astounding. One would have supposed that by putting two and two together, and repeating the operation a few times, Mr. Baker might have reached the same conclusion without being admitted to the "inside." What must be the feeling of those who have mastered the technic of military art, those army chiefs who, as Secretary Baker has also discovered, are not spoiling for war but are simply trained and thoughtful men who feel responsible for a cer-

---

[1] From an interview by Fred C. Kelly, published in *Harper's Weekly* for April 22, 1916.

tain branch of the national service—what must be their feeling as this new scholar publicly recites his alphabet with all the airs of profound insight!

A policy of adequate military preparedness is not, except for those few persons who profess non-resistance, a question of principle, but of prudence and expediency. To be converted to it, it is only necessary to learn by experience, to observe facts and make inferences, and to govern one's present actions by a sane regard for future contingencies. In other words, it is merely a question of being normally intelligent about the hazard of war. Even universal military training is, I believe, dictated by mere prudence, quite apart from the wholesomeness and fairness of having the duty of defense undertaken jointly by all whose interest is at stake.

There is gradually unfolding[1] in England a most impressive, and, to all friends of England, a most distressing object-lesson in the failure of the voluntary system. This system creates the very resistance that it has to overcome. Events have proved, it seems to me quite unmistakably, that there is no real choice between compulsory service and voluntary service, but only between compul-

[1] Written in March, 1916.

sion in advance, as a part of the deliberate policy of the state, and compulsion in the midst of the national crisis. In the latter case it is too late to be fully effective, and is imposed unexpectedly upon those who are by elimination the most unwilling to serve, and who have been taught to believe that compulsory service is contrary to the political principles under which they live.

Granting universal military duty to be the effectual as well as the democratic way of doing what must be done, it follows that it is reasonable to make a virtue of necessity. And here it is proper to argue the educational benefits of military training. That such benefits do accrue, no one who has had the least experience will deny. Prompt obedience, the economy of time, power to work effectively with all sorts of men, the ignoring of minor vexations and discomforts, self-sufficiency as regards the elementary things of life, physical health and endurance, manual expertness—these are some of the lessons that are *learned* in the school of war. They are not carried away in note-books but under the skin in nerve and muscle. The greatest lesson of all is the habit of thinking nationally, the feeling that one has a country, and that one owes it something. A man then makes the acquaintance of his country as a whole, and for once, at least, looks it in the face.

Now there are doubtless other ways in which this national-mindedness may be cultivated. Professor Dewey has proposed the centralization of the educational system, and Mr. Walter Lippmann has proposed the government ownership of railways.[1] It can be urged against any of these proposals, including that of universal military training, that it implies the existence of that very national-mindedness which it is supposed to promote. There is evidently a circle that has got to be broken somewhere. A general national policy, foreign and domestic, for peace and for war, in education and in economic life, will develop rapidly when once the federal authority is an object of loyalty and confidence; and when on its part it serves the people with greater foresight, with a broader grasp of the total situation, and with a more serious sense of responsibility. But this new state of things cannot be certainly achieved by any single act or propaganda. No man can tell where the existing habits are weakest and may most easily be overthrown, or what may appeal most vividly to the imagination of the people. If educational and economic reform

[1] *The New Republic*, for February 19 and April 15, 1916.

can break the circle, by all means let them go forward. Meanwhile the spectacular tragedy of war, and the sudden necessity of thinking politically upon the larger international scale, have already done much to arouse us from our separatism and complacency. There is a spreading belief that if we are to take part in the making of history we must acquire the strength to do it. Military training, or some other exercise to make oneself fit for national service, is a natural outgrowth of the desire to *act* in this great crisis when every good thing is in jeopardy. It may well be that this emergency will enable us to find ourselves; and that from marching together, or working together to make the nation strong, we shall get a new sense of comradeship and of partnership that shall in the end revolutionize our culture and our social order.

But it is neither the necessity of military service, nor the virtue that may be made of this necessity, with which I want here more especially to deal. Military service has also its attendant dangers. I urge them not as arguments against it, but as abuses to be avoided. If there is any institution that is an unmixed blessing, I have never heard of it. It is not religion, for example, or conscience, or art, or government. Every

political or social policy has its dangers; democracy itself has, perhaps, the most insidious dangers of all.   But we do not abandon such policies
when we have reason to believe that they are
necessary, or are the most hopeful alternatives
open to us.   We adopt them, and then seek so
far as possible to offset the attendant dangers.
This we can do all the better for being put on
our guard.

So in the case of universal military service I
shall summarize its dangers not in order to throw
them in the balance against it, but in order to
suggest positive measures by which these dangers
can be avoided.   If as a nation we are to take up
arms, or even exercise ourselves in their use, it
must be with a certain solemnity.   Arms are
edged tools; they are not playthings.   If we are
to acquire their use we must learn to use them
safely, and only for a serious purpose.   We must
take measures to prevent their abuse, and to
safeguard the superior interests which they might
otherwise injure.   Their use must be adjusted to
those ends that justify our national existence.
Military service should not only be dedicated to
the highest end within the range of our present
moral vision, but it should be informed with
whatever human quality we think is finest, and

corrected or offset by whatever measures may effectually protect our liberties and minimize the inevitable sacrifice.

There never was a greater need than now of a comprehensive policy. The vivid fact of war and the new historical crisis have already upset our equilibrium—despite every attempt on our part to hold aloof. New national policies are inevitable, and have, in fact, already been inaugurated. It is necessary, therefore, as though we were moving into a new house in a more thickly settled neighborhood, to see to it that there are rooms for all the family, places for our possessions, and shrines for our gods. In particular, how shall we be as strong as the hazard of war requires with the least prejudice to our peaceful pursuits and our constructive humane ends? It is the importance, here and now, of such a stock-taking and reckoning of cost that will justify, I hope, the rehearsal of familiar truisms.

1. The American army should both be dedicated to the service of democracy, and also be itself an example of democracy. Democracy is on trial, as it has been many times before. Usually the jury has disagreed. The charge has always been the same, namely, that democracy implies a lack of organization which breeds lawlessness,

corruption and weakness. Just now it is a question whether a democracy can survive. Can it unite with liberty, equality and fraternity, enough strength to enable it to hold its own among governments which enjoy a greater concentration of power, and which can avail themselves of general habits of subordination and obedience? Can a house be governed by discussion without being divided against itself and suffering the proverbial penalty? The future alone holds the answer. But this much is evident—that unless a democracy can be strong it cannot be said to have succeeded at all. Therefore, whoever devotes himself to democracy must seek ways of making it strong. He who neglects the question of military preparedness fails not only to solve the problem of democracy but even to grasp it. A democratic government must be able to do what other governments do, namely, provide security against attack from abroad, and the necessary mechanism and organization by which the nation may exert its united strength when occasion requires. A democracy which relies for the execution of its policies on the indulgence or accidental interest of other nations, is a confessed failure. If, for example, we wish to defend Belgium against Germany but have to call upon France to do it for us; if we avow the Monroe Doctrine but trust that if it comes to blows the English fleet will help us out; then our government has failed, whatever liberty of speech and thought we may enjoy in our domestic affairs. To prove that a democracy can maintain itself, protect the interests under its charge, and be as good as its word, is then the service which the armed force of a democracy owes to the cause of democracy.

Like all of the agencies of the central government the military organization is in danger of spreading the error that the state is an end in itself. The symbols of war, the flag, martial music, the rhythm of parade, all of these tend to beget an idolatrous worship. Democracy is founded on the principle that the authority of government is justified only by the benefits which accrue to the governed. Democratic patriotism is not a blind and slavish loyalty, but is mixed with a strain of intelligent self-interest and providence. A democracy must not allow its head to be turned by drum-beats and gold braid. The real business of life is still to promote the happiness and well-being of individual men and women. The agencies of war as well as those of peace must be regulated and rigorously judged with reference to this end. The mere emotional effervescence of the war spirit must not be allowed to create "The Great Illusion," or any other illusion by which men are prevented from recognizing where their interest lies. Though the immediate object of military loyalty must be the state, that object must not in a democracy be worshipped by a devotee who asks nothing in return, but rather prized by one who well understands its beneficence.

If the army and navy are not to subvert the democracy for which they act, they must be democratic in their own internal spirit and organization, without loss of discipline.[1] This is by no means impossible. It was achieved by the French armies of 1792; and, if we are to trust the reports, has been again achieved by the French armies of to-day. A football team is not less democratic for its team-work or for having a captain. Each individual member of the team feels that he depends on all the rest, and that it is necessary that there should be some one to lead and give commands. He who leads

---

[1] The critics of universal service are as a rule silent regarding the objections that can so easily be urged against a professional army. A hired army is neither so representative, nor so responsible, nor so voluntary in its service as a citizen army. There is a very forcible discussion of the matter in F. S. Oliver's *Ordeal by Battle*, part IV, chap. VII.

and he who is led both play indispensable parts and serve the same end. So in a democratic army the officer and the private are comrades because, each doing something needful, they acknowledge one another's support in the common cause. The officer is not a person who enjoys privileges so much as one whose duties are more exacting and more responsible. He is less distinguished by his trappings than by his long hours. He is more bound than the private, who looks to him rather with gratitude than with envy.

Responsible leadership and prompt concerted obedience are not undemocratic where they are pervaded by an understanding of the game, and the will to play one's part in it. They become undemocratic only when the difference between officer and private coincides with more generally recognized social cleavages. To avoid this it is necessary that officers and men should be recruited from the same social classes, so that superiority of military rank should be identified only with superiority in military skill, or with that native quality of leadership which is independent of breeding or culture. It is important that men of wealth and position should serve in the ranks, and that men who are favored only by their military experience and native fitness should rise from the ranks to command them. To the same end it is important that humiliating punishments should be avoided, and the authority of officers confined within clearly recognized bounds, so as to protect the self-respect of privates from the abuse or caprice of authority. In short, a democratic army must owe its discipline to morale and loyalty, rather than to harshness and to fear. It is self-evident that there is most hope of fostering this spirit in an army of citizens conscious both of the equal dignity and of the common service which that rôle implies.

In his famous essay, "On Liberty," which is still the best specific for paternalism, Mill says that a free people must be "accustomed to transact their own business." He cites the resourcefulness of the French in times of revolution as being due to their military experience and the presence everywhere among the people of men who have been non-commissioned officers, and who have therefore a capacity to lead and to organize a plan of action. He attributes to Americans a like resourcefulness "in every kind of civil business," and contrasts France and America with the bureaucracy in which "all the experience and practical ability of the nation" has been organized "into a disciplined body for

the purpose of governing the rest." A free people
must be a people in which potential leadership
is everywhere widely diffused; in which all have
some aptitude both to command and to obey.
The personnel of the military organization should
therefore be in some degree interchangeable.
There is an obvious military advantage in this
because it creates an inexhaustible reserve of
officers. But the deeper reason for it lies in its
divorcing the office from the man, and substi-
tuting a subordination of position for personal arrogance and abasement. It should serve also to
keep alive within the breast of one who has become for the time a colorless unit in the ranks
the peculiar temperament of an individual and
the high pretensions of a man. In short, a democracy must avoid a military caste, which it can
best do by making the people its own army; and
it must avoid an official caste, which it can best
do by flexibility of organization, frequent promotion from the ranks, the interpenetration of
all social classes in all grades of service and the
promotion of a sense of partnership and personal
equality between those who command and those
who obey.

2. Universal military service is consistent
with democracy only in so far as it is popular.

The principal objection to the so-called voluntary system is the fact that when compulsion is at last used, as it inevitably is, it is without the support either of the habits or the judgment of the people. The constitutionality of compulsion is not disputed. Every government must at least hold it in reserve as a course of last resort. In any war with a nation of equal or superior power, it will always be probable that the voluntary system will prove inadequate. The only way of avoiding the ugly method by which after the more willing have first been drained away the more unwilling residuum is then threatened and coerced, is to adopt the policy of universal service from the outset, with open eyes, because of its utility and its justice. It is then possible to create habits of mind and of body that are really consistent with national needs.

The success of the policy in this country, as in England or any other democracy, must depend on the attitude of the working classes. There is reason to hope that organized labor may be converted to the principle of national service, not only from motives of patriotism, but for its educational and social advantages, and for its possible indirect bearing on economic difficulties through the creation of a better understanding between the working man and his employer. It is also probably inevitable that universal service should lead to the state's assuming on its side a greater responsibility for the welfare of the working classes. In short, a more provident and constructive economic policy might well grow out of the more vigorous nationality, and the more vivid sense of co-operation and mutual dependence, that universal military service would stimulate.

3. Whatever system of military service this country may adopt must be suited to our peculiar institutions and to whatever we account indispensable to our national temperament. It has been argued that *any* military system is contrary to the genius of America. We are reminded of those who came here to escape military service, and to whom America would not be America were it not for that immunity. Now it is dangerous to identify national life merely with immunity. Men will go anywhere to escape a disagreeable duty. That they should come to America from that motive argues no devotion to American institutions and promises no willingness to assume the responsibilities of citizenship. It is a misfortune that America is reputed to be a land where you can make money easily and do as

you please. Those whom this repute brings to us are likely to feel abused when they find that here as elsewhere success requires work, law and taxes. Compulsory military service is in principle contrary to no ideal save that of reaping without toil and sacrifice; which is a delusion on which no national life can be founded.

That which is most necessary in order to adapt military training to American life is that men should, as in the Swiss system, be withdrawn only for short periods from civil life. The function of war must always be regarded as subordinate to peaceful pursuits, in the life of the individual as well as in that of the nation. The citizen must be a non-combatant first and a soldier second. He must derive his tastes and standards from his family, economic, political or recreative associations, so as to prevent the development or dominance of a distinct military type. Occasional military training, the attainment of skill in arms and manœuvres, need no more suppress individuality than do athletic sports. The military uniform need no more efface personality than does the civilian uniform. As a matter of fact, uniformity in unessentials, such as clothes, step, carriage or manual dexterity, is a means by which one may escape attention and therefore be permitted to pursue one's own way in essentials, without scrutiny and censorship. Long hair and a flowing cravat bespeak not that independence which Americans respect, but that ostentation and tenderness to social regard which Americans are inclined to find ridiculous. If there be anything in military form which is contrary to our spirit it is not that unobtrusive and workmanlike uniformity which is important, but those decorations and other concessions to personal vanity which can more easily be dispensed with.

4. It is essential to democracy that the civil authority should be superior to the military authority, and that there should be one law and one moral code for soldiers and for shoemakers. What happened in Zabern in 1913 ought to be intolerable among Americans. The civilian control of our military forces is provided for in our constitutional forms and is heartily seconded by public opinion. We must be content even with a loss of efficiency rather than run the risk of military rule. Policy must at all times be governed by the electorate, and criticism of authority must always be tolerated so long as it is intended as an appeal to the arbitration of public opinion. Even in times of war it is essential to a democ-

racy that the great body of citizens should exercise their political prerogatives. It is not incon-
sistent with soldierly duty that one should fight
so long as a state of war exists, and yet vote for
a policy that would terminate the war.

If there be any fear that an American army
once organized on a formidable scale might be
employed for aggressive purposes by an ambitious
or unscrupulous administration, it is always possible that compulsory enlistment should be confined to service at home, or on the borders. By
such a provision a man would incur less risk of
being ordered to do that which in principle he
disapproves. He would not have given himself
unconditionally into the keeping of another; but
would have adopted the service freely from the
imperative ground of national safety. It is impossible to deny, however, that such conditional
service might at times defeat the purpose of defense. "The only question of real importance,"
says Mr. F. S. Oliver, "is this: At what place
will the sacrifice of life be most effective for the
defence of the country? If we can answer that
we shall know also where it will be lightest." [1]

It has been urged against compulsory service,
by Mr. Norman Angell, for example, that it re-

[1] *Ordeal by Battle*, p. 403.

quires a man to fight in a war he deems un-
righteous, and stops him from criticising it.
That any given individual should be free at all
times to do as his conscience dictates is somewhat less possible in time of war than in time of
peace. But the difference is only one of degree.
Authority of any kind, civil or military, implies
that individuals shall do under pressure what
they would otherwise not do. If a man is un-
fortunate enough to be a conscientious nihilist
or a conscientious polygamist, he will find himself constrained to act contrary to his own best
judgment. He may have conscientious scruples
against paying his taxes, or against educating
his children, or against submitting to vaccination.
But the state will penalize his action without
respecting his conscience, and if he incites to riot
on behalf of his own peculiar ideals he may have
to submit to martyrdom. No way has been
found nor ever will be found of avoiding this
tragedy; it is simply the price which is paid
for the benefits of social order. But this tragedy
is minimized under liberal political institutions
by permitting individuals at stated times and in
stated ways to share in the making of the laws
under which they live. Under such institutions
there are measures which a man may legally

take toward making the law more to his own liking. But meanwhile he must obey it as it is—under protest, if he wishes.

In principle precisely the same situation exists in war-time. If the nation is in fact at war, then the executive and military authorities must prosecute that war as effectively as they can under such laws or rules as may exist for their guidance. A citizen who does not approve of the war must bide his time. He has had his opportunity to influence national policy, and he will have it again. Meanwhile, he must bear his share of the burden which the national exigency imposes. Whether he be a volunteer or a conscript will not much matter. He cannot expect to reserve liberty of action in the presence of the enemy. If his conscience is offended, so much the worse for his conscience. What he needs is a new conscience which will teach him to keep the faith with his fellows until such time as their common understanding and their controlling policy shall have been modified. The man who refuses to obey the law or play the game because he has been outvoted is more likely to be afflicted with peevishness or egotism than exalted by heroism.

Under a system of national service, furthermore, the army and the electorate are one and the same.   In proportion as the government is popular, the army will itself have authorized the policy under which it acts.   Unpopular wars are much less possible under such a system than under that system in which war is voted by one man and fought by another.   When war means to each voter his own personal obligation to abandon peaceful pursuits, submit to hardship and risk his life, he will interest himself in foreign policy, and will not lightly lend his support to an aggressive or to a quixotic enterprise.

5.   Since military service itself emphasizes the central authority, increases solidarity and promotes loyalty to whatever is traditional or established, it is important that it should be offset by agencies tending to independence, individuality and criticism.   The greatest of these agencies is education.   Over and above the education for livelihood and the education for service, it is indispensable that there should be the education that emancipates.   There could be no greater disaster in a free country than that a national educational system should be contrived merely to mobilize the intellectual and moral resources of the community for the purposes of the state. Co-operation, patriotism and all the civic virtues must indeed be imparted, but without killing

that revolutionist and non-conformist that lives within every free man's breast. Nationalistic education must never displace that "universal" or "personal" education which Goethe said only noblemen enjoyed in his day, but which in a democracy must be open to all eager minds.

6. If war is not to be the result of caprice or accident, if it is not to be forced upon one unexpectedly by the aggression of another nation, it must be subordinated to some general international policy. As has been rightly insisted, military preparations can be rational only when they are supplemented by some statesmanlike and far-reaching plan of action. The present war is rapidly destroying our traditional domesticity. The American policy has in the past been a home policy, such as the securing of independence, the winning of the West and the preservation of the Union. The Monroe Doctrine, if it is to survive, must be put upon a new international basis. That we must henceforth live among nations was a heresy yesterday, but to-day it is only a truism. It is as true of a nation desiring to be let alone, as of one cherishing dreams of conquest. For the future a nation can as little afford to be without an alliance as a man can afford to be without a country. That isolation

which was once our strength is now our weakness.

7. A liberty-loving country like our own should bring its rustic virtues into the international society. It is possible to be cosmopolitan without being cynical. There is no reason why we should not be diplomatic without being arrogant. There is a courtesy which reconciles pride with generosity, and enables self-respecting individuals to pay honor without inquiring too particularly whether it is due. Similarly there is a mode of national conduct which permits of national convictions and national purpose without loss of humor and tolerance. Let us, therefore, cultivate this spirit of reciprocating and chivalrous nationality.

8. The political principle by which international relations may be rescued from lawlessness, but without offending against the just pride of individual nations, is federalism. Fortunately it is more than a principle; it is already an achievement. The integrity of the British Empire under the strain of war is the most hopeful political sign of the time. It is the most triumphant realization which history affords of that "co-existence of several nations under the same State" which Lord Acton a half-century ago said was "one of the

chief instruments of civilization,"[1] and indicative of greater advancement than the mere unity of a single state. The loyalty of the self-governing British dependencies, each with its strong local pride and ambition, with its individual differences of social organization, temperament, language and race—their instant recognition of a common crisis and a common cause, affords better ground than any event of history for the hope that all nations may some day be federated. World-wide federation means one state for international purposes, together with autonomy for national purposes. It means the rallying of all nations to the defense of the international authority and policy, while that policy, in turn, promotes the diversity of national cultures, and enables each nation to prosper in its own way. As Mr. H. N. Brailsford has well insisted, no international league can flourish simply "by force and threats."[2] It must promise advantages. Nations must be persuaded that they can gain their own ends best in the settled neighborhood of nations, rather than on its lawless outskirts.

The problem that arises from the contrast between more advanced and more backward peoples

[1] *History of Freedom and other Essays*, p. 290.
[2] *The War of Steel and Gold*, p. 330.

has its only chance of solution through the same principle. Somewhere there must be a frontier where strangers meet; where they must learn to be friends if not enemies, and to trade if not to plunder. The world cannot exist half savage and half civilized. There is a genuine difference between a savage and a foreigner, between a Hottentot and a Chinaman. The one is to be educated or protected as a child; the other to be regarded, if not with understanding, then at least with respect, as another way of being a man. The obligation of civilization to savagery is that of helping it to its feet, without directing where it shall walk. We shall have done our work well in the Philippines if we have taught those who live there how to be different from ourselves, and how to do it well. If we were to force our culture upon them, and convert them, for example, to the literary school of Bret Harte, Mary E. Wilkins and James Whitcomb Riley, we should commit an impertinence, and impoverish the world. But if we can show them how to keep the peace among themselves and with others, how to find their own resources and develop their own capacities, and then leave them to perfect themselves in their own way, we shall have helped a brother and created a new nation.

9. He who takes up arms must enter the service of peace. This is not a mere paradox, or the echo of a prevailing sentiment, but honest downright morals. Universalism must take precedence of nationalism on the same ground that entitles nationalism to take precedence of individualism. Nationalism is a higher principle of action than individualism, by all the *other* individuals of whom it takes account. A nation is not a mystical entity, other than you and me, but it is more than you or me inasmuch as it is both of us and still more besides. Similarly, humanity is more than nationality, not because it is different, but because it is bigger and more permanent. No man, least of all a soldier, can ignore any of the effects of his conduct. He must promise himself that his conduct shall in the final reckoning be helpful rather than hurtful. He must have imagination and intelligence enough to judge his action by its effects across the boundaries of his nation and of his time. If he be thus enlightened he will then justify himself only when his action, though in its first incidence it be destructive, is in its full effect a saving and multiplication of life.

III

THE TOLERANT NATION

WORDS sometimes owe their usefulness to their ambiguity. Thus, one's doubt or utter blankness of mind when compelled to pass judgment on a work of art is decently concealed by such words as "interesting" or "suggestive." The commonest word in the technical philosophical vocabulary of any age is usually a label by which some part of the primeval chaos is neatly covered so that attention may be concentrated on the rest. Just now it is the word "experience." In contemporary political thought a similar service is rendered by the term "nationality." It is a commonplace of recent history that the nineteenth century was peculiarly a century in which men fought and argued in terms of the principle of nationality. The present war is supposed to be due to the assertion of nationality, and justified by the defense of it. But just what nationality is, is far from clear. Indeed, most discussions of the matter are chiefly concerned to show that it is not any of those things which it is usually supposed to be.

44

Thus, a nationality is not the same thing as a state. This is clear, whatever one's view as to their relative priority. If we are to believe Lord Acton, "a state may in course of time produce a nationality; but that a nationality should constitute a state is contrary to the nature of modern civilization."[1] According to this view nationality may arise from "the memory of a former independence," and its principal cause be tyranny and oppression from abroad. But even so, the nationality once acquired is a different thing from mere political independence. It is a new fellow-feeling begotten by political adversity. It does not consist in the mere fact of a common government but in the new sense of common loyalty and common proprietorship. Similarly, when it is argued that nationalities should be granted political autonomy, it is assumed that they may exist in its absence. Thus the Austro-Hungarian Empire is commonly described as a single state composed of many nationalities. Or when it is proposed that a world-state should be formed out of existing nationalities, it is taken for granted that these nationalities as such would in some sense maintain their identity.

The fact is that with the growth of liberal polit-

[1] *History of Freedom and other Essays*, p. 292.

ical thought it has become less and less possible to regard the state as an ultimate by which nationality or anything else can in the last analysis be explained. Once the state is divorced in principle from the de facto government, or from hereditary legitimacy, or from the sanction of the church, it must be supposed in some sense to express the collective needs and aspirations of a social group. And in so far as the citizens of any state so regard their government, as theirs to adopt, or to make and mould, it is evident that the state becomes, if it was not originally, an instrument and visible sign of something like nationality. This, of course, does not explain what nationality is; but only discourages the hope of identifying it simply with the state, and points to the necessity of looking to the deeper facts of social solidarity.

There are certain solidifying agencies that are evidently not so much criteria of nationality as conditions necessary or favorable to its existence. Thus it is evident that a nationality is not an ethnological unit. Neither purity of race nor even a common racial blend defines such a nationality as our own; although it is evident that racial homogeneity conduces to national life and is in some measure invariably present. It is doubtless

the most powerful single cause of group unity.
Similarly, men who, as Nietzsche says, "speak one
language and read the same newspapers" are in
so far qualified for common nationality, since
they are capable of intercourse and share a common literature. But since languages are so easily
learned and so easily forgotten, and since the same
language can be spoken by peoples otherwise remote
and diverse, this evidently affords neither a fundamental nor a sufficient principle of nationality.

Propinquity is evidently a necessary condition
of the neighborly relations and co-operative action implied by nationality; but the boundaries
of nationalities only occasionally follow physio-
graphic frontiers. A common climate or other
aspect of nature will give to a local group a
sense of identity not unlike that which the individual derives from the "feel" of his own
body; but most national territories embrace too
much variety to find in this a general bond. A
common past and common traditions evidently
solidify a group just as his peculiar memories
give to each individual a sense of his personal
uniqueness. But there are new nations as well
as old; and in any case it is not the mere fact of
historical continuity but its cultural effect which
is significant for nationality.

In short, race, language, physiography and history do not constitute nationality, but conduce to it in so far as they give rise to the sense of a common life. It is evident, then, that national individuality like personal individuality is a psychological fact which has many varying and supplementary causes. A man will possess nationality in so far as he identifies himself with a group by act of will and a less conscious but not less significant community of sentiment or idea. Although the difference is not a sharp one, and although the two factors act and react upon one another, it will be useful to distinguish between the bond of *utility* and the bond of *culture*. I shall therefore consider nationality under each of these aspects and endeavor to bring to light in each case the causes by which nationality tends to tyranny and intolerance, or the means by which this evil consequence may be prevented.

The bond of utility means simply that every individual finds it expedient to go into partnership with his fellows. He must attach himself to some organized society in which his interests are adjusted to those of other men according to certain rules which are defined and enforced by a common authority. Nationality in this sense is the same as polity, but only provided polity

is regarded as a voluntary association for mutual
benefit, and not as an alien coercive force. The
state is an expression of nationality only in so
far as it is adopted and acknowledged as their
own by a group of participating beneficiaries.
There is, of course, a wide difference of opinion
as to the scope of this political partnership, rang-
ing from laissez-faire to state socialism. But
there are two benefits which are the least that is
expected of the state: the benefit of internal
peace, and the benefit of security against external
aggression. A state is a social group living under
one system of law, and making common cause
together against dangers from abroad. A state
has one police, and one military force, ruled by
one ultimate authority. This account of the
state ignores such ambiguous situations as have
been created in the past by the temporal claims
of the church, and such as are created now by
federal systems and by alliances. These doubtful
cases prove that it is impossible to distinguish
the identity of the state in any absolute and un-
qualified manner; but they do not affect the
particular considerations to which I wish now to
turn.

The internal or domestic policy of a state defines the limits within which individuals may do

as they please without getting in one another's way. Its object is to secure to each individual as large a sphere of liberty as possible; in short, to guarantee private privilege. Variety, originality, happiness and growth are the signs of its success. These things must, however, be attained by organization and discipline. And therein lies the difficulty and paradox of domestic policy. Repression and orderly routine are indispensable; but if carried too far they defeat their purpose. There is such a thing as a sort of national asceticism in which repression is deemed an end in itself, instead of an instrument of liberty. Organization is an art and requires experts; but these readily become a bureaucracy and eventually a ruling class which asserts its own interests in place of those it was designed to serve. "Whenever a single definite object is made the supreme end of the state," to quote Lord Acton once more, "be it the advantage of a class, the safety or the power of the country, the greatest happiness of the greatest number, or the support of any speculative idea, the state becomes for the time inevitably absolute." [1] In other words, whatever the function which the state exercises, it requires submission. But this

[1] *Op. cit.*, p. 288.

submission may become a habit through confusion of mind or through helplessness, so that the instrument becomes a burden and a tyranny. Hence the just suspicion of authority which is characteristic of the peoples of western Europe and America. Hence "eternal vigilance is the price of liberty." Here is the danger which justifies the distrust of representatives and experts among the more advanced democracies— the rude insistence that public officials shall be servants, and that if experts be necessary, then all must be educated to some competence in public affairs.

But this same characteristic difficulty is aggravated by the interplay of domestic and foreign policy. A common danger from abroad outranks in urgency any question of domestic rights, as in the case of the individual the question of life or death instantly eclipses questions of comparative happiness. Thus the threat of war invariably leads to a conservative reaction. It has led, in France before the war, and in all countries since its outbreak, to the postponement or slighting of such questions as the relations of church and state, or the extension of the suffrage, or the improvement of the conditions of labor.

It is, moreover, unhappily the fact that the policy which best serves individual interests at home, and the policy which makes a nation most powerful abroad, do not coincide. A liberal domestic policy implies protest and insubordination; it encourages claims and counter-claims in behalf of private interests, and leads to changes of the existing equilibrium. Power abroad, on the other hand, implies concentration of purpose, a forgetfulness of grievances, and a willingness to bear injustice in the presence of the great emergency. Thus the solution of the great problem of personal happiness and development is retarded or put aside, and society returns for a time to the rudimentary question of bare preservation.

I do not for a moment mean to belittle this question of preservation. It does and must take precedence of other questions. Aggression from abroad creates a genuine emergency. In order that nations shall be anything at all, they must first exist. Even such apprehension as has led Englishmen of to-day seriously to advocate a dictatorship is not wholly groundless. The tragic fact is that no people can give itself up whole-heartedly to the improvement of the lot of individuals, or to any of the higher spiritual purposes of civilization, until all peoples are engaged in the same task. A single aggressive

power let loose in the world can compel all nations to be on their guard, and so to devote to
the end of barely living, energies that would
otherwise be devoted to the task of living better.
Nations like individuals require a guarantee of
security before they can afford to be happy. The
problem of civilization is therefore a common
and a mutual task in which all nations must
move abreast. The national virtues that are
required in an age of international lawlessness
contradict those more liberal virtues to which
civilization aspires. But the latter imply the
advent of a new era in which international authority shall have delimited a sphere within which
each nation may live out its life in safety and
freedom.

So much, then, for that illiberality in national
life which is due to fear, that invoking of the
principle of force which is necessary in order to
meet force on equal terms. But this necessity
is due to aggression which must somewhere arise
from within. Such aggression may be and commonly has been due to motives of utility—to the
desire for land, natural resources, or other economic advantages. Without belittling the actual effect of these motives, I wish, nevertheless,
to ignore them in the present discussion in order

to emphasize another motive which is more novel and more distinctive of the present crisis. I refer to the motive of national culture. This is the present warrant of aggression when aggression takes high ground. Its danger lies in its self-righteousness. We know what to make of honest, straightforward aggrandizement, and we know what to call it. But the nation which goes forth to conquer not only in shining armor, but with shining faces all aglow with the sense of a holy mission, is not only a menace to life and property, but to reason and conscience as well. One stands aghast with one hand on one's pocket and the other on one's troubled brow.

Culture as a bond of nationality, is a very different matter from the culture that liberalizes and emancipates. It is *a* culture, a peculiar system or code of beliefs, sentiments and customs, by which a people feel themselves to be in some measure distinguished and set apart. Mazzini said that those who aspire to nationality "demand to associate freely, without obstacles, without foreign domination, *in order to elaborate and express their idea.*" [1] A national culture is an idea or system of ideas, as to how to live and as to what is worth living for, common to the

[1] Quoted by J. Dover Wilson, in *The War and Democracy*, p. 16.

members of a group and peculiar to the group as a whole. Such a special culture arises from a thousand causes, many of them obscure, but it does arise and get itself recognized.

This is not that quaint affair of "sweetness and light," or knowledge of "the best that has been thought and said in the world," of which we have more often heard. It is not that cosmopolitan value which is associated with art, science, philosophy and history. National culture is in a certain respect the precise opposite of liberal culture. Thus science is a part of liberal culture in so far as it deals with nature, employs a dispassionate method and arrives at generally valid laws; but science is a part of German culture in so far as it is performed by German scientists and applied to German economic life. Art is a part of liberal culture in so far as it implies generally valid standards of taste and makes one family of Phidias, Dante, Shakespeare and Goethe; but it is a part of German culture only in so far as it creates a *Denkmal* of Bismarck, or in that Goethe happened to be born in Frankfort-on-the-Main, or in that Shakespeare's dramas are appreciated in Berlin. In liberal culture philosophy began with Plato because he was "the spectator of all time and eternity," in national culture it began with Kant because he lived in East Prussia. History in so far as it is an affair of culture, enables one to inherit the whole empire of the past. As a part of German culture it enables one to trace one's descent from a select family of barbarians who dwelt in the Pomeranian bog.

It is evident that the culture-motive in nationality may readily become a source of illiberality. But since some measure of common sentiment and opinion is both inevitable and desirable, it is important to discover precisely wherein this danger lies. Its source will be not in the fact of national culture, but in the attitude which accompanies it. It is not in being German, for example, that the danger lies, but in being too self-conscious about it, or in taking it too seriously.

There is a good deal of nonsense abroad in the world, aided and abetted by a certain type of philosophy, as to the value of self-consciousness. It is very easy to confuse originality and distinction with the use of the looking-glass or the first personal pronoun. As a matter of fact the man who possesses individual distinction is far more likely to be absorbed in an object or cause than in himself. If he departs from usage it is because he is really careless of appearances, not

because he is studiously careless. In the latter
case one is aping the appearance of carelessness,
and so conforming to a type. He is endeavoring
to be what is expected of him, not what he is
prompted to be by his own peculiar genius.

The same thing is true of national distinction.
In so far as it is indigenous and original, it is
unconscious and not self-conscious. It comes of
exercising one's judgment honestly and indepen-
dently. The way to be American, for example, is
not to play a character-part representing the conventional "American traits," but to seek the best,
or do one's duty as one sees it, leaving the Americanism to take care of itself. If one is born in
America, if one lives in the American milieu, subject to the characteristic influences of that environment and tradition, the Americanism *will*
take care of itself. National movements in art,
science or philosophy are not the result of men's
trying to be French or English; but they result
when Frenchmen or Englishmen try to make
something that is beautiful or say something
that is true. No important cultural movement
in the world's history has resulted from the deliberate cultivation of one's own peculiarities.
On the contrary they have usually been inspired,
as in the case of the Italian Renaissance, by a

somewhat extravagant regard for the peculiarities of others. That which distinguishes the motive of great art and science is its universality,
its objectivity, its preference of standards to
personalities or local pride. The personal or
national quality, like the quality which distinguishes an epoch or a race, is determined by
the angle and point of origin from which the
universal is approached, and it depends for its
fullest expression, not on self-consciousness, but
on absorption and sincerity.

But self-consciousness is worse than a weakness by which the purpose of national culture
defeats itself. Not only does it divert the attention from the greatest and best things, and
check their liberalizing and quickening power,
but it begets a state of self-righteous irresponsibility that is a positive danger to the rest
of mankind. National self-consciousness, like individual self-consciousness, emphasizes the form
rather than the substance of life. It breeds
irresponsibility because it encourages men to
believe that the agent's end of the act is more
important than the patient's. If the agent feels
or conducts himself in a certain prescribed manner,
then it matters little what the consequences of
the act may happen to be. The good marksman

is the one whose form is good, not the one who hits the target. Moralities of this sort are common enough. There is the conscience school which teaches that the criterion of right action is the inward oracle rather than the outward effect. This school has been too conventional, too wedded to the conservative moral tradition to be as dangerous as some others. Even so, its blind conservatism and its bigotry are well-known. The full danger of this way of thinking is realized when it is united with the radical temper. Any act has virtue, says Nietzsche, which issues from the sense of power. If you can feel masterful while you do it, it doesn't so much matter what you do; you may even perform deeds of benevolence.

But the great morality which has emanated from Germany is that of "self-realization." The important thing according to this view is that your deeper self should act, and not some momentary impulse. When you deliberately choose an act, or put your whole self into it—when it is really *you* that do it, with a full sense of the gravity of this self-committal, then the act is a right act, whatever comes of it. Of course, it will be a part of your deliberation to take the consequences into account. But that will be incidental to the coaxing out of the deeper self, and will never prove the act right or wrong. Now, it is clear that this doctrine is readily applied to the case of nationality. The precept, "Be yourself," may, when one identifies oneself with the nation, be amended to read "Be German," or "act so as to feel German when you do it." The act will then be right, because it was rightly conceived at the source.

There is a danger for the agent himself in such a sanction of conduct. It gives rise to the mistaken belief that one can sow without reaping, and so encourages a fatuous disregard of the laws of life. It is like the medicine by which some persons hope to offset the effects of gluttony, or the piety which is warranted to save one's soul without requiring that one shall mend one's ways. But the greatest danger of formalism is that which threatens not the agent but the unhappy mortal on whom he chooses to realize himself. A man with a conscience, or a sense of mastery, or a self, or some other inner authority by which he justifies himself, is a menace to any neighborhood. He is like a man playing with dangerous weapons, who doesn't look where he is shooting. For every act is a dangerous weapon. Discharged in the midst of a thickly settled community it is sure to hit and injure somebody, unless its direction and effects are carefully regulated. It wouldn't do in any community to allow men to discharge loaded firearms simply in order to express themselves. Or if it were permitted, the most dangerous man would be he who felt he had the most to express.

So society finds it necessary to suppress any man who is too exclusively concerned with being himself, and has to be especially firm with those who take themselves seriously. When spiritual exaltation reaches a certain height it becomes necessary to use handcuffs and a strait-jacket. If a Nietzschean superman should break into any settled community he would of course have to be jailed at once. National self-consciousness has to be met in the same way by the neighborhood of nations. The justification of action by its expressiveness of national peculiarities, a policy dictated simply by the principle of being one's national self, whether German or anything else, is socially intolerable. It has to be regulated, or even suppressed, in the interest of public safety.

A national culture may, then, be intolerant by virtue simply of a heightened self-consciousness—an excessive self-preoccupation. This motive is not primarily aggressive. The effect upon others is not so much calculated as disregarded. But it is easy to pass over into a sense of self-importance or into the conviction of a holy mission. Self-importance may simply argue youth. There is something of this doubtless in present German nationalism. It is a new nationalism, and is so important to those who have recently achieved it after a long struggle, that it is easily assumed to have cosmic importance. Such youthful self-importance is naturally associated with self-consciousness; as in the case of the young man with his first pair of long trousers, for whom all windows are mirrors. But this German self-importance is a deeper and more formidable thing, which can be traced back even to the age before the Napoleonic wars. From Kant's day to the present, Germans have been exhorted to believe themselves peculiarly indispensable to civilization. This was at first doubtless a counsel of despair. When Fichte said to the German nation, "If you sink, humanity sinks with you," he sought to restore the self-respect and determination of a people prostrate before the conqueror. But in the long run the German nation has believed what it was told, and has no intention of allowing humanity to sink. On the contrary,

Germany proposes to make the elevating of humanity its particular business and whether humanity likes it or not. There is a dreadful seriousness about it, a resoluteness of purpose which may well cause the unregenerate to tremble.

To understand the precise nature of this cultural mission it is helpful to consult the familiar analogy of religion. It was only after painful struggles that the mind of western Europe was emancipated from the conviction that it is of the essence of religion to be intolerant. This was because the mind of western Europe had become thoroughly habituated to the Jewish and Christian idea that the God of a particular historical tradition was Almighty God. According to the pagan idea the god of any special cult must necessarily be a particular god—that is, only one of many gods. The only common God is the divine principle at large, which cannot be monopolized, but only worshipped by each people according to their lights and under such forms and manifestations as their special interests and locality shall dictate. A religious cult of this sort protects its own gods from sacrilege, while also admitting the sacredness of other gods. But Judaism and Christianity have said: "*Our God*, the God of our fathers, the God we worship and proclaim, is *the* God." It is sacrilege to the Christian God to admit the sacredness of any other god, and the benefits of religion are in this view denied to all save those who associate themselves with the chosen cult. It therefore becomes the mission of this cult to save men in the name of "true religion" from the religions they freely choose. Hence the long tragedy of intolerance and persecution, with its diabolical paradoxes—the use of force to impose belief, the violent assault upon piety from the motive of piety, the grim resolve of one man to do good to his neighbor even though his neighbor should die of it, and die cursing his self-appointed benefactor.

Now if for religion we substitute civilization, and if for a special cult like Christianity we substitute a national culture, we discover the parallel which I wish to emphasize. Civilization like religion has its special dispensations, and there are two views that one may take of that dispensation under which one lives. One may do homage to it, and at the same time respect the diverse prejudices of others; or one may believe that one's own dispensation is the exclusive channel through which the blessings of civilization are to be distributed to all mankind. In this case alien prejudices become a sin by which men destroy their chance of progress, and from which they must be saved for their own good. Thus Germany presents the remarkable spectacle of a modern nation which regards itself as the chosen people of civilization; chosen to save the world, not in the world's way, but in its own, the German way. This is neither localism nor universalism, but both; the clothing of this particular thing that flourishes here and now, with the awful authority and majesty of the absolute. It has precisely the same effect upon the uninitiated as though a familiar companion were suddenly to say: "Oh, by the way, you know *I* am *God*." Such a remark at once renders social relations impossible. If one believes, then one may bow down and worship. Otherwise, one must either fly for one's life or employ forcible restraint.

A cultural mission, like an intolerant religion, justifies itself by a philosophy of history. Indeed, most philosophies of history consist in giving absolute metaphysical significance to the historical moment of the author, or in picturing history so that it converges upon the author. In this the German philosophies of history have imitated the Christian models of Saint Augustine and Saint Thomas. Thus for Hegel art culminates in Romanticism, religion in Lutheranism, and politics in the Prussian monarchy. The modern world is "the German world," simply. But this is only a retrospective view of the matter, and is comparatively harmless. The more sinister motive finds expression in Kant's view of patriotism as the will that the end of humanity "shall be first realized in the particular nation to which we ourselves belong, and that this achievement *thence* spread over the entire race." [1] The extraordinary thing is this proprietary interest in civilization. It is as though one claimed a sort of concession in perpetuity to bottle the essence of civilization and sell it under a trade name.

Bernhardi would not be significant if he were original. In claiming "all the intellectual and moral progress of mankind" to rest on the achievements of Luther and Kant, he is simply quoting tradition. The same is true of the striking passage that follows, and which Professor Dewey cites with effect in his admirable book, *German Philosophy and Politics*.[2] The tone of this passage is in harmony with that of the founders of spiritual Germany. "To no nation except the German," says Bernhardi, "has it been given to

[1] Quoted by J. Dewey, in his *German Philosophy and Politics*, p. 99.
[2] P. 35.

enjoy in its inner self 'that which is given to mankind as a whole.' . . . It is this quality which especially fits us for leadership in the intellectual domain and imposes upon us the obligation to maintain that position." As we outsiders, the prospective beneficiaries, listen to these words we know how the oysters in *Alice in Wonderland* felt toward the weeping carpenter; or how the keeper feels toward the embraces of a friendly elephant; or we remember how we ourselves once felt toward the stern parent who told us that it hurt him worse than it hurt us.

The spectacle of coercive benevolence visited by one adult of the species upon another, may afford laughter to the gods; but that is because they happily dwell in a safe place where no one seeks to do them good. For the hapless object of benevolent intent it is a grim business. And since it is natural to benevolence to expand and to be untiring, it is inevitable that a general uneasiness should pervade the whole family of nations so long as any one of them is thus inspired and dedicated. It is not only a dangerous thing, it is an inherently tragic thing like a great mind gone wrong. Cultural intolerance, the sense of a national mission, is a morbid excess of virtue.

It is divided from the best and greatest things by a few degrees of more and less. It implies resolute purpose, self-respect, subordination to a cause. Its contempt for others, its consciousness, is like the hardness of a man who cannot be indulgent to others because he expects so much himself.

La Mettrie said that an invisible fibre would suffice to make an idiot of an Erasmus. It may take a cerebral lesion to cause mental paranoia, but moral paranoia may be caused by something even less evident and ponderable. A little difference of attitude, scarcely to be remarked at all save in its effects, makes the difference between seriousness and censoriousness, between idealism and fanaticism, between loyalty and bigotry, between zeal and aggression. The crucial attitude which thus preserves moral sanity is a recognition of one's own fallibility, a sense of humor regarding oneself. It is humor that sweetens nationality, as it sweetens individuality and keeps it from spoiling. There are not many things that a man may not say if he will occasionally betray by a smile, or by the look in his eye, that he knows how it sounds from your point of view. It is scarcely possible for national pride and self-love to be too great, provided it be accompanied by the saving grace of

self-criticism, and by a general sense of a something so much bigger than oneself as to make
comparisons ridiculous. Nations, like individuals,
need perpetually to recover their sense of proportion by reminding themselves of their liability to
error, or of their need of all possible light from
all possible sources on those questions which are
so great as to be almost hopeless.

Tolerance springs from a recognition of one's
own limitations, from the feeling that there is
too much to the truth, or to civilization, for any
one group of men to fathom or compass. Such
is the spirit of Mill's plea for individualism:
"That mankind are not infallible; that their
truths, for the most part, are only half-truths;
that unity of opinion, unless resulting from the
fullest and freest comparison of opposite opinions,
is not desirable, and diversity not an evil, but a
good, until mankind are much more capable than
at present of recognizing all sides of the truth,
are principles applicable to men's modes of action, not less than to their opinions. As it is
useful that while mankind are imperfect there
should be different opinions, so is it that there
should be different experiments of living; that
free scope should be given to varieties of character, short of injury to others; and that the

worth of different modes of life should be proved practically, when any-one thinks fit to try them."[1]

The just relation between independent nations is precisely that which underlies the higher forms of intercourse between independent individuals. Friendship, rivalry, commerce, war, discussion, partnership, may all be ennobled by this relation. It consists in mutual respect. It is much more than an affair of manners. It means that each acknowledges in the other that power of judgment and self-determination, in which his own manhood consists. As each judges for himself and devotes himself with resolution to what he deems good, so he recognizes the same finality and self-sufficiency in others. He respects in others what he respects in himself, and since he receives respect from the object to which he gives it, he can be respectful without ceasing to be self-respecting.

In essentials the same relation must underlie the intercourse of nations. Each believes in itself, and judges by its own standards. But this very loyalty and resoluteness will create an admiration for the same quality in other nations. It is as though one nation were to say to another: "Your ways are outlandish, and your judgments wrong, but I doubt not mine seem equally

[1] *On Liberty*, chap. III.

so to you. Which of us has the better of the argument, God only knows. We believe that we have, but we enjoy no peculiar immunity from error. Perhaps we can persuade you that you are wrong. Perhaps it will turn out that we are both half right and half wrong. Meanwhile there is room for us both if we are willing to make it."

Such a national spirit conduces, like Mill's individualism, to a rich variety of type, and to the mutual aid of many minds, each trying its own experiments and attacking in its own way the common problems of civilization. It is an indispensable condition of any peace save the peace in which arrogance dominates slavishness. If nations, like individuals, are to be allowed any pride or belief in themselves, or the courage of their convictions, then if there is not to be perpetual war, there must be a general spirit of tolerance —a willingness to respect what one cannot agree with or even understand.

But tolerance is not to be prized merely as a means of diversity or of safety; for it directly elevates the tone of national life. A man is seen at his best when associating with those he regards as his equals. Sycophancy and superiority, servility and mastery, conduce equally to the warping of character. The man who can enjoy intercourse only with his superiors or inferiors, who must play the toady or the bully, and does not know how to look any man horizontally in the eye, is morally defective. So the finest quality of national life is reserved for those nations which can be faithful to themselves without loss of sanity. Such nations will not be restrained by force from oppressing their neighbors. They will rejoice in the existence of their neighbors, and will doubly rejoice in finding their neighbors worthy of their mettle. They will feel in the intercourse of proud and differing nations the same zest that is felt by a man among men.

When peaceful rivalry or friendly co-operation takes the place of war, this attitude will be no less needed. For that same mutual respect which may ennoble even war, is all that will save peace from a spirit of easy acquiescence, or from a mean contentiousness. Peace itself has to be redeemed, and that which alone will save it will be an eager championship of differing national ideals, a generous rivalry in well-doing, the athlete's love of a strong opponent, and the positive relish for diverse equality.

IV

IMPRESSIONS OF A PLATTSBURG
RECRUIT

IT is a mistake to suppose that a soldier's impedimenta are merely accessory. From the time when you first gratefully borrow them from the ordnance and quartermaster's tents to the time when you still more thankfully deliver them up, you revolve about them. In place of the ordinary organic sensations, they supply while you possess them the nucleus of the consciousness of self. Though much is made of the ceremony, there is really no credit in returning these objects to the United States Government. The real merit is in borrowing them at all. This is perhaps the bravest act a soldier is called upon to perform. There are, let it be understood, some twenty-five separate articles in this borrowed equipment, including half a shelter-tent, one rifle, one canteen, one poncho, five pegs, etc., and to these one is ordered to add articles of toilet and personal apparel, bringing the total

number to over thirty. These, when once you
have put them together, you acquire as a part of
yourself, like a permanent hump. They *might* be
folded, hooked, and strapped together in a thousand ways; they *must* be folded, hooked, and
strapped together in one way, and in only one
way. And then they must be taken apart again,
and combined anew for each day's journey;
which is one of the most successful of the several
standard devices for protecting the soldier from
the corrupting influence of leisure.

When you advance upon an imaginary enemy,
your corporal, whom you have learned to watch
as a dog his master, shouts "Follow me!" You
are wearing your hump, with its various outlying
parts, such as the rifle in your hand and the canteen on your hip. By bending your body until
your back is parallel with the ground, you are
able to simulate running. The gait as well as
the contour resembles the camel's; but alas! you
enjoy no such natural adaptation for pack-bear-
ing, nor for the rude contacts with earth that
await you. For after loping forward some twenty-
five yards, you are ordered to "lie down."

This is not to be construed as an invitation to
enjoy a well-earned rest. On the contrary, your
torture is about to begin. In civilian life it is

customary when lying down to select some spot or object which yields slightly to the pressure of the body, or corresponds somewhat to its outlines. But in skirmish formation you lie down in your place; if you are a rear-rank man, then half a pace to the right of your file-leader. The chances are one hundred to one that the spot fits you very badly. Nevertheless, down you go. You then hoist up on your left elbow, and address your rifle in the direction of the enemy. Your whole consciousness is now concentrated in the elbow. This member, which was never intended as an extremity, rests in all likelihood upon a rough-edged piece of granite separated from your bone by one thickness of flannel shirt. The rifle presses mercilessly upon it. Your pack, thrown forward in your fall, rests upon the back of your neck, adds itself to the weight upon your elbow, and renders it almost impossible—judged by civilian standards, altogether impossible—to look along the sights of your rifle. The pain in the elbow is soon followed by a sharp cramp in the wrist. When these parts have become sufficiently numb for you to attend to minor discomforts, you begin to realize that you are lying on your bolo knife, and that your canteen is sticking into your right hip.

At this moment the platoon leader orders you to "fire faster," and with a desperate contortion you reach around to the small of your back and grope for a slip of cartridges with which to reload your rifle. Then "Cease firing!" "Prepare to rush!" and again "Follow me!"—this time not only *to* a prone position, but *from* a prone position. You are carefully enjoined that you must get up running and lie down running, lest you shall at any time present a fixed target to the enemy. You dig a hold with your foot, summon your last reserves of strength, totter forward with all your goods hanging, dangling, dragging about you, and soon resume business with that elbow exactly where you left off. This is called "advancing by rushes," and it is customary to do it for distances of a thousand yards or more in instalments of fifty yards or less. It is capped by a bayonet charge in which after drawing the reluctant bayonet with the right hand from just behind the left ear, and fumbling hastily about for the proper grooves and sockets, you expend your last ounce of strength in a desperate sprint up-hill.

Now in this description I have made no reference to the enemy. In fact there is no reference to the enemy, at least no personal reference. There is a vague sense of the enemy's direction, described as "twelve o'clock" if it be immediately ahead, or "one o'clock" if it be a little to the right, etc. But you entertain no murderous thoughts except for the person, luckily unknown, who invented your pack; and you are not apprehensive or sorry for the enemy, for you are too profoundly, too whole-heartedly sorry for yourself.

In all this there is a most extraordinary alteration of one's scale of values. I think I can understand something of the mind of the soldier in the trenches who welcomes the order to stand erect, preferring the chance of death to another moment of agonizing cramp. At such times remote memories and prospects, the normal hopes and fears of life, are expelled by importunate sensations. One is either too acutely wretched, or too gloriously happy, for either anxiety or regret. The range of consciousness is narrowed to aches and pains, or to such soul-satisfying joys as full respiration and restored circulation.

There are compensations in hardship, wholly unsuspected by those who have not lived through them. To stretch one's limbs without a pack, to sit by the roadside against a bank, to drink lukewarm water out of an aluminum can, to eat beans out of a tub, to bathe by hundreds in one shallow brook, to mitigate the natural roughness of one's stubble bed with a bit of straw—it requires some cultivation to raise these experiences to the pitch of ecstasy.   But it is worth while.   When, in decorous society, one is informed that "Dinner is served," it is in apologetic and doubtful tones, as though the announcement were intrusive or unwelcome.   But with what glad emotion does one spring forward, unashamed, with mess-kit extended for instant use, when one hears the hearty roar of the Falstaffian undershirted cook: "E Company!   *Come* and *git* it!"

There is a popular belief that it is a fine thing to be an officer, or even a "non-com."   And it is doubtless important that this belief should be professed in training camps.   But volumes might be written confidentially on the luxury of being a private.   When, in one of the occasional lulls between the stated exercises of the day, some sergeant shouts down the company street, "Squad leaders come and get ammunition," or "Non-commissioned officers report at the first sergeant's tent," then if you are a private there steals over you the delicious realization that it does not mean you.   It is like sick-call when one is well.   I despair of making an uninitiated person realize the full significance of an order that does not mean you. Your poor corporal scurries out of the tent, you hastily take possession of the much-coveted ramrod which he has been forced to leave behind, and then and there, thanks to your corporal's harder lot, you enjoy a genuine sense of leisure. Not that you do nothing—only exhaustion justifies that. But you clean your gun with a cosey feeling that you have got at least that day's work well in hand.

Let me hasten to add that cleaning your gun does not mean the same thing as making your gun clean. It means an infinite series of motions approaching cleanness as a limit which they never reach. Each rag seems to come through the muzzle blacker than the last. The captain calls special attention to screw-heads and other minute cavities, and you poke individual grains of sand about in them with the point of a pin; but you never get them all. The simple child-like faith with which this task of Sisyphus is performed is touching. It becomes in time a sort of harmless mania, a chronic activity which one automatically resumes whenever not diverted by more urgent business.

Corporals and sergeants enjoy no immunity from rifle-cleaning, pack-carrying, or any of the thousand duties that keep a private on a panting dog-trot from reveille to taps, and since they are burdened with other duties as well, their lot is hard. The worst of it is that they have to think and make decisions. At least they have to try, which is just as bad. But the last thing that is wanted of a private is that he should have ideas of his own. Even when in doubt as to his orders, a private who is fully alive to his prerogatives will ask his corporal, and wait patiently and restfully for him to find out. The great thing is that a private can, by an adroit passivity, both earn praise for his soldierly obedience and at the same time ease his mind. With his body he has to be everlastingly at it, and there is no escaping that pack. But the non-commissioned officer is a pack-animal who is required also to think—an unparalleled cruelty; while the commissioned officer, if he has less on his back, has so much the more on his mind. Oh, the luxury of the vacant mind! Oh, the restfulness of the obedient and incurious will! Oh, the deep peace of hooking the canteen under the fifth right-hand pocket of the belt, without having to decide between the fourth or the fifth, or inquire why it should be either!

Soldierly experiences are common experiences, and are hallowed by that fact. You are asked to do no more than hundreds of others, as good or better than yourself, do with you. If you rinse your greasy mess-kit in a tub of greasier water, you are one of many gathered like thirsty birds about a roadside puddle. If you fill your lungs and the pores of your sweaty skin with dust, fellows in adversity are all about you, looking grimier than you feel; and your very complaints uttered in chorus partake of the quality of defiant song. To walk is one thing, to march, albeit with sore feet and aching back, is another and more triumphant. It is "Hail! Hail! the gang's all here," or "Glorious! Glorious! one keg of beer for the four of us"—it matters not what the words signify, provided they have a rhythmic swing and impart a choral sense of collective unity. Special privilege and personal fastidiousness, all that marks one individual off from the rest in taste or in good fortune, seeks to hide itself. Instead there is the common uniform, prescribed to the last string and button, the common nakedness of the daily swim, the common routine, the common hardships, and in and through it all the common loyalty and purpose.

To many this is the first dawning consciousness of the fellowship of country. Patriotism is not praised or taught, it is taken for granted. But though inarticulate, it is unmistakably the master motive. There is a fine restraint in military ceremony that enables even the purest product of New England self-repression to *feel*—without awkwardness or self-consciousness. Every late afternoon at the last note of retreat, the flag is lowered, and the band plays "The Star-Spangled Banner." Men in ranks are ordered to attention. Men and officers out of ranks stand at attention where they are, facing the flag, and saluting as the music ceases. Thus to stand at attention toward sundown, listening to solemn music sounding faintly in the distance, to see and to feel that every fellow soldier is standing also rigid and intent—to experience this reverent and collective silence which forbears to say what cannot be said, is at once to understand and to dedicate that day's work.

V

THE FACT OF WAR AND THE HOPE OF PEACE

RADICAL pacifism and radical militarism both rest upon a one-sided view of the great human problem of international polity. In coming to see the error of both of these forms of propaganda, we shall, I believe, approximate to something like a balanced and adequate view.

Radical pacifism may be said to contain two ideas, non-resistance and neutralism. Non-resistance is commonly confused with unselfishness. As a matter of fact, however, under present conditions it would mean saving one's own skin and one's own feelings while others' suffered. No one will dispute the right of an individual to submit passively to abuse, provided he receives the abuse upon his own person. There may even be a certain dignity in such non-resistance. An individual may be "too proud to fight"—for himself. The real test of the principle comes when you apply it to the defense of those you love.

No man should announce himself an advocate of non-resistance who is not prepared to acquiesce in the violation of his wife or daughter. No woman can be at heart non-resistant unless she means that she is willing to surrender her child to torture. No American can renounce the appeal to arms unless he can think with equanimity of the extinction of his race or the crushing of those institutions which now stir his civic pride and loyalty. For these are the evils which an attacking enemy may seek to perpetrate, and which defensive warfare aims to forestall. The enemy's will in the matter cannot be controlled. It takes two to make peace, but either party may at his own discretion threaten the other with the blackest evil which his imagination can invent. He may force upon whomever he elects to be his enemy the dilemma of armed resistance or of submission to any outrage that his victim may deem most unendurable. To be non-resistant must mean, then, that one regards nothing as unendurable—even the destruction of what one loves or admires or has sworn to serve and protect.

There is a theory that non-resistance will soften arrogance and disarm brutality. This theory is based upon the extension to group actions and emotions, of influences that may occasionally be exerted by one personality upon another. Collective non-resistance evokes only contempt. The effect of non-resistance when practised by a whole race or nation is unmistakably apparent in the history of the Jews and of China. A caste or conquering race that is accustomed to the meekness of inferiors grows hard and arrogant. Unless in the last analysis men or nations are ready to fight for their honor and their treasures, material and spiritual, they raise up enemies whom they invite to despoil them. Those are respected who possess reserves of rugged determination, who wear a quiet and unconscious air of willingness to defend with their lives whatever they hold to be priceless—their goods, their country, their friends, their loved ones, their lives, or their principles.

The other idea which distinguishes radical pacifism is neutralism. This means refusing to take sides, reserving judgment in the presence of the great struggle. It manifests itself in the present crisis in the attitude of those who declare that all parties are equally to blame or equally innocent. It is an easy-going policy, for it saves the pain of decision and permits the mind to muddle along in a state of flabby vacillation and procrastination. The present crisis is like every great political and social crisis in that it is the resultant of many forces, which it takes hard thinking and clear seeing to disentangle. If one is to stand aside because a problem is complicated one may as well go into a hermit's cell and be done with it. To be effective in this world is to hazard a judgment and to commit oneself to it.

The worst of it is that neutrality may so easily become a habit and render one permanently hesitant and weak. It begets indifference, when it does not spring from it. If one cares much for one's flag one will find it flying somewhere and follow it. Furthermore, those who proclaim neutralism as a part of the creed of pacifism forget that the possibility of permanent peace depends upon the cultivation of sentiment and opinion. It is absolutely impossible that there should be a public opinion strong enough to secure peace, which shall not be terrible to those who disturb the peace. One cannot hate lawlessness and brutality without hating those who perpetrate or instigate them. To be tolerant of manifest and present evil is to emasculate one's moral consciousness. In that future time when state war is as exceptional as private war is to-day, it will be necessary that a lawless state shall be visited with the same resentment and swift condemnation that is now visited upon the lawless individual. When, therefore, one seeks in the name of peace to suppress the strong sentiment that is widely felt against that nation which surpasses all others in violence and cruelty, one is counteracting the very force by which one's cause may hope some day to triumph.

Non-resistance and neutralism are the false friends of peace. They bring disrepute upon it. There can be no propaganda that is effective and morally sound which requires one to yield weakly to hostile attack, or to emasculate one's judgment. If there be any excuse for these excesses in the name of peace, it is the like tendency to exaggeration which marks the exponents of war.

False or radical militarism is also characterized by two ideas. The first of these is the belief in the necessity or institutional character of war. Plato, as a matter of course, divided his Republic into warriors, merchants, and guardians. He regarded war as a natural function of the political organism, and the warrior as the embodiment of spiritedness and courage. But we are now coming to the view that war is a disease to which the race is peculiarly liable in its infancy, and from which it may hope to secure immunity in its maturity. War is now known to be natural not in any final or ideal sense, but in the sense of being crude and primitive.   It is one of the things that civilization seeks not to perfect, but to outgrow and put aside altogether.

Viewed in this light, the soldier is the symbol not of human attainment, but of affliction and painful necessity.   He is as much out of place in the perfected society as the rat-catcher or the policeman.   The cost of war has grown unbearable, and is now reckoned more accurately.   Its effects have grown more fatal in proportion as social organization has grown more elaborate and more delicately adjusted.   Its essential clumsiness and wastefulness, its swift and prodigious destructiveness, are intolerable in an age devoted to constructive and progressive civilization. Meanwhile its methods have so altered that it has almost wholly ceased to be an art or a romantic adventure which may appeal to the amateur or which a man may follow as a polite vocation.   It is even ceasing to possess a code of honor.   It is ugly, sordid and prosaic, offensive to taste and repugnant to humanity.

We have also come to understand that the propensity to war is not incurable.   It is not necessitated by any law of human nature.   Even were self-interest the law of human nature, that law would dictate peace and not war. For security is more profitable than lawless aggression, and property is worth more than plunder. But self-interest is *not* the law of human nature. There are instincts of neighborliness which increase in their range as news and travel increase the circle of one's neighborhood. There are some instincts, it is true, which lend themselves to warlike uses; and owing to an accidental emphasis in psychological theory, we have recently heard much of them. But though there be an instinct of pugnacity, there is no instinct of war. War is only one of divers ways in which the instinct of pugnacity may find expression. One may be equally pugnacious in the interest of saving souls or eradicating disease. One may even be pugnacious in the cause of peace. For just because pugnacity is an instinct, it is modifiable and plastic. Not only is it balanced by other and contrary instincts, but it does not issue in conduct until it has assumed the form of habit, purpose or conscious will. Man has instincts, but he is not possessed by them. He is called an intelligent or rational being because he can check, regulate and guide his instincts by the light of knowledge and direct them to the good ends that his judgment may adopt.

A fatalistic acquiescence in war, the acceptance of it as permanent and inevitable, is the first sign of the radical militarist. The second is suspicion or misanthropy. Within certain limits it is an almost unfailing rule of human conduct that we shall receive from men what we manifestly expect of them. He who goes about with scorn or truculence or cold suspicion written on his face will find it reflected in every face he sees. He who does not expect to be spoken to will find himself cut by his acquaintances; the man of cold reserve will find himself living in a community of snobs. On the other hand, a child wins kind words and kind looks because he so unhesitatingly and confidently assumes that he is going to get them. The misanthrope thinks that he finds confirmation of his opinion from the facts, whereas in reality he causes the facts himself.

A like phenomenon appears in the relations of nations. Suspicion begets suspicion; suspicion mounts to hatred, which begets hatred; while all the time a different original attitude might have stimulated a latent kindliness or called attention to common interests and so have led to a habit of friendship. Mischievous gossip may do much to create artificial enmities between one man and another. Between nations this danger is magnified by the difficulty of obtaining news, and by the possibility that the very instrumentalities of news may be used to provoke and foster enmity. There is therefore need of a good will that shall not only be cordial and resolute, but that shall accord the benefit of the doubt. There was never greater need of such an attitude than at the present time, nor a better application than our relations with Japan. A sneering contempt for the motives of others, a quickness to believe malicious or chance rumors when they agree with the creed of selfishness, and to charge every profession of disinterestedness with insincerity— nothing could be better calculated than this to suppress whatever impulses to generosity, candor and cordiality our human nature prompts. Such an attitude is neither enlightened nor humane. It is a persistent belief only in the worse possibilities, and so is unscientific; it acts as a restraint upon the better possibilities, and so is mischievous.

Such are the extravagances of a false pacifism and of a false militarism. In so far as they are committed to these extravagances both propagandas must be rejected. It is an intolerable dilemma which forces one to choose between being a sentimentalist and being a reactionary. The great majority of thinking men must decline to be either. The association of both propagandas with their extravagances tends to a state of hopelessness and inaction, and obscures the real problem. It is necessary to move forward in this matter, as in all other great affairs that involve collective action, by a series of steps that shall secure new benefits without forfeiting old. What all men must desire to secure is a durable peace without loss of liberty, honor or self-respect. Any plan by which one buys off one's enemy by the surrender of independence or principle is wholly beside the point. By tame submission to allow any belligerent to have his way is to confirm him in his creed of lawless aggression. On the other hand, to fall back blindly on the old shibboleths of nationalism and patriotism is to acknowledge the failure of civilization. It follows that nations must so fight for their liberties and their principles as to bring that day nearer when it shall no longer be necessary to fight for them.

There is a wide-spread impression that there is something incompatible between these two attitudes, the acceptance of war as a deplorable present necessity, and the pursuit of peace as a glorious hope. But there is no such incompatibility. On the contrary, such a mixture of expediency and idealism is one of the most familiar and universal facts of life. That which distinguishes constructive progress from mere pious wishing is the use of present means to bring one forward toward one's end. The present means will always be of that age which one seeks to leave behind. It is necessary to walk until one can ride, and to ride until one can fly. It is only the fanatical mind which fails to see so obvious a fact, or to govern itself by a principle so fundamental and so indispensable to all forward action.

I submit, then, that we need a propaganda that shall take the middle ground, and recognize the real problem. In place of war parties and peace parties that exaggerate their own half-truths, and ignore all other half-truths, thus blinding our eyes and impotently consuming our passions and energies, we need the wise and balanced mind, adjusted to the needs of the hour and inspired with hope of the future.

Persons so minded will agree that there is war in fact, and that so long as there is war there is danger. Where there is danger any thoughtful mind must commend caution and foresight, so that the danger may be well and effectively met in proportion to its imminence and its magnitude.

But it is no less imperative that the hope of peace should be kept bright and that the purpose to attain permanent peace should be undaunted. Prophecy and inspiration are as important as efficiency and trained judgment. It is no less important to contrive new social and political devices and to agitate for their application and trial. Projects for disarmament, for an international court, or for the publicity of diplomatic negotiations, should not be regarded as vain imaginings because they depart from ancient practise, but as inventions by which after trial and selection men may eventually forge the tools by which to establish a new and better practise. In short, the upward road of progress can be ascended only by one who both keeps his footing secure, and looks ahead with ardor and imagination.

VI

WHAT IS WORTH FIGHTING FOR?

NOT long ago a newspaper despatch from
Leicester, England, described the untimely
fate of a travelling band of pacifist preachers who
styled themselves "The Fellowship of Reconciliation." It appears that the good patriots of
Leicester beat them soundly, burned their camp
and equipment, and concluded the matter by
singing "Tipperary" and "God Save the King"
over the ashes.

The incident epitomizes the absurd but deeply
tragic plight of man. His bravest and most exalted purposes, those of nationality and humanity, are driving him to self-destruction. There
is more of tragedy in this than a present loss of
life and material goods; there is a dreadful sug-
gestion of doom, as when one first detects symptoms of an incurable disease. There is a seeming
fatality in life by which right motives impel man
to work evil. Intelligence, self-sacrifice, devotion to a cause, those qualities of mind and will

on which we have been taught to pride ourselves, seem only to make men more terrible, or more weak, according as they turn to deeds or to meditation. To take up arms and destroy, or to sit passively by while destruction rages unrebuked—there is apparently neither virtue nor happiness in either course. If such be the predicament of man, it is not surprising that many are praying that the curtain be rung down and an end made of the whole sorry business.

In what I have here to say I address those who are still determined to think the matter through notwithstanding the fact that, as Mr. Tulliver says, "thinking is mighty puzzling work." Despair we may reserve as a course of last resort. Likewise the death-bed consolations of religion by which human weal and woe are left to the inscrutable wisdom of Almighty God. When the present scene becomes too painful we may shut our eyes, or turn to some celestial vision. But I for one cannot yet absolve myself from responsibility. There is a task of civilization and social progress to which man has so solemnly pledged himself that he cannot abandon it with honor. And in this hour of trial that pledge requires us to form a plan of action which shall be neither an act of blind faith nor a confession of failure.

We must endeavor both to see our way and to make our way.

How shall the constructive work of civilization be saved and promoted? It would be a much simpler matter if it were only one's "inward peace" that was at stake. Mr. Bertrand Russell tells us that "the greatest good that can be achieved in this life is to have will and desire directed to universal ends, purged of the self-assertion which belongs to instinctive will." [1] But there is one greater good, and that is the *accomplishment* of these universal ends. This is a much more baffling and hazardous undertaking. It requires a man not only to make up his mind, but to bring things to pass. It becomes necessary to use the harsh and dangerous instruments by which things are done in this world. Civilization is not saved by the mere purging of one's heart, but by the work of one's hands. The forces of destruction must be met, each according to its kind, by the forces of deliverance. The belief that when a man has struck an attitude, and has braved it out in the midst of a rough and vulgar world, he has somehow solved the problem and done his duty, underlies much of the pacific sentiment that is now abroad. It is a

[1] *Atlantic Monthly*, August, 1915, p. 267.

dangerous error, because it makes the difficulties of life seem so much simpler than they really are, and may teach a man to be perfectly satisfied with himself when he has really only evaded the issue.

For what does this philosophy of inward rectitude really mean and imply? In the first place, it is self-centred and individualistic. Life becomes an affair between each man and his own soul, a sort of spiritual toilet before the mirror of self-consciousness. Social relations only furnish occasions for the perfecting of self, trials by which one may test the firmness of one's own mind. The state, economic life, and other forms of co-operative association, lose their intrinsic importance, and tend to be replaced by a select fraternity of kindred spirits, in which each is confirmed in his aloofness from the vain hopes and petty fears of the world of action.

The crucial test of such a principle of life is afforded by the presence of a danger which threatens *others* whom one may be pledged to serve, or some larger good extending beyond the limits of one's personal life. Whether to save one's *own* peace of mind at the expense of one's *own* life or property is a question which may well be left to the individual to decide for himself.

But as so often happens, this relatively simple question is also relatively trivial. Such a choice is rarely if ever presented. Certainly the emergency in which war arises is never one which a sympathetic and imaginative person can meet merely by applying the scale of his own personal preferences. It is not one's own person that is imperilled. As a matter of fact it requires the most colossal egotism to suppose that the enemy has any interest whatever in one's own person. It is the collective life, the state, the national tradition and ambition, the chosen and idealized civilization, the general state of happiness and well-being in the community—it is these that are in danger, and it is these that one must weigh against one's private tranquillity.

If the matter be viewed in this light, it is a little absurd to step forward and gallantly offer one's life in exchange for being allowed the privilege of dying innocuously! Such an offer will sound heroic to no one but oneself, and to oneself only in so far as one has lost both sympathy and imagination. It is doubtless vexatious that one cannot be allowed to choose for oneself alone, but such is the hard condition of life. When one chooses to take up arms or to suffer the enemy to triumph, one is disposing, not of oneself, but of all those lives, possessions and institutions which the enemy threatens and which it lies within one's power to defend.

But the philosophy of inward rectitude is not merely self-centred, it is also formal and prudish. It is pervaded with a spirit of correct deportment. Its aversion to war is largely due to a feeling that war is banal, and incompatible with the posture of personal dignity. The philosopher's cloak must be thrown aside if one is to adopt the graceless and immoderate gait of the soldier. War is intolerable, just as running is intolerable to one who has come to enjoy the full measure of self-respect only when he is permitted to move with a slow and rhythmic strut.

But this is the antithesis of the spirit of enterprise. Genuine devotion to an end, intently working for it, will render one unconscious of the incidental movements and postures it involves. A formalist would not lie on his back under an automobile, because such an attitude would not comport with a preconceived model of himself as an upright, heavenward being of a superior order; whereas a traveller, bent on reaching his destination, would not shrink even from the aboriginal slime, if only he might find a way to go forward. Similarly if it were all a matter of propriety of demeanor, one could refuse the ugliness of war and shut one's eyes to the sequel. But if one's heart be set on saving civilization, so laboriously achieved, so fragile and perishable, then one's personal attitude is contemptibly insignificant. All that really matters is the fidelity with which one has done one's work and kept one's trust.

Nor will it suffice to quote Plato, and take comfort in the thought that the ideals are themselves eternal and incorruptible. For that which enemies threaten and champions defend, is not the ideal itself, but some earthly, mortal thing which is made in its image. The labor and art of life is not to create justice and happiness in the abstract, but to build just cities and promote happy lives. And these can be burned with fire and slain by the sword. If one is prepared to renounce the existent world and the achievements of history, one may perhaps escape the need of war. But let no man fail to realize that he has then virtually given up the whole creation of the race, all the fruits of all the painful toil of men, even the spiritual fruits of culture and character. For these spiritual fruits are individual lives which may be as utterly destroyed as the work of man's hands.

It is futile to argue that the good life cannot

be destroyed by an enemy. It is true that it cannot be corrupted, and made evil. But it may be killed. The good life is more than mere goodness; it is *living* goodness, embodied in existence and conduct. He who slays a just man or annihilates a free and happy society, undoes the work of moral progress as fatally, nay more fatally, than he who corrupts them with injustice and slavery. For in the latter case there at least remain the latent capacities by which civilization may be rebuilt. Those who insist on the distinction between might and right and accuse the warrior of practising might in the name of right, are likely on their part to forget that the work of civilization is to make the right also *mighty*, so that it may obtain among men and prevail. This end is not to be realized by any philosophy of abstinence and contemplation, but only by a use of the physical forces by which things are brought to exist and by which alone they are made secure against violence and decay.

Having considered the philosophy by which men avoid war, let us now consider another philosophy by which men make war, with an equally easy conscience and an equally untroubled mind. I refer to the philosophy of nationalism:

the worship of the individual state as an end in itself, and the justification of conduct solely by the principle of patriotism. Such a creed may be idealized by a belief that the ultimate good lies in the progressive strife of opposing national ideals; a strife which is humanly discordant and tragic, but is rounded into some sort of all-saving harmony in the eternal whole. Practically this makes no difference except to add to the motive of national interest the sense of a heaven-sent mission. The only end by which the individual is required to judge his action is that of the power and glory of his own state. To that is merely added the dogma that national conquest and aggrandizement are good for the world even if the poor world doesn't know it. By such a dogma a people whose international policy is unscrupulously aggressive may enjoy at the same time an ecstatic conscience and a sense of philosophical enlightenment. Hence this is the most formidable and terrible of all philosophies. Its devastating effects are manifest in the world to-day.

There are two fatal errors in this philosophy. The first is the assumption that the state is something apart from the happiness and well-being of its members. The state, contrived to serve men, becomes instead, through tradition, prestige and its power to perpetuate its own agencies, an object of idolatrous worship. Under its spell free men forget their rights, wise men their reason, and good men their humanity. The second error is the dogma that the narrow loyalties of nations will best serve the universal good. There is no evidence for this. It is the joint product of national bigotry and of an ethics manufactured by metaphysicians. The experience of the race points unmistakably to the fatally destructive character of narrow loyalties, and teaches the need of applying to national conduct the same standards of moderation, justice and good-will that are already generally applied to the relations of man and man.

There is one further way of evading the real difficulty of our problem, but this can be dismissed with a bare mention. I refer to the flippant and irresponsible scepticism which holds all human purposes to be equally valid because all are equally blind and dogmatic. The sceptic views with mild derision the attempts of man to justify his passions. He holds all nations to be equally at fault, equally self-deceived, and equally pitiful. The folly and discord of life do not surprise him, for he expects nothing better than that man should consume himself. On such a philosophy war and peace are not to be seriously argued, but accepted as fatalities, whose irony affords a refined enjoyment to the emancipated mind.

These, then, are the philosophies of evasion and irresponsibility. Before accepting any of them it behooves one to be clearly conscious of what they imply. It is impossible here to argue these deeper questions through. It must suffice to point out that all of these philosophies are opposed to the beliefs on which modern democratic societies are founded. Unless we are to renounce these beliefs, we must refuse in this grave crisis to listen to any counsel that is not hopeful and constructive, that does not recommend itself to reason, and that does not define a program of universal human betterment. When such a solution is firmly insisted on, the real difficulties of the problem appear. But though one may well be troubled to find the way, one may at least be saved from the greater evil of self-deception.

There is no fair escape from the tragic paradox that man must destroy in order to save. Never before has this paradox been so vividly realized. Man goes forth with torch and powder to restore the primitive desolation, and to add to the nat-

ural evils—from which he has barely escaped—
more frightful evils of his own contriving. He
does this in the name of home, country, humanity and God. Furthermore, he finds himself
so situated that neither conscience nor reason
permits him any other course. His very purpose
of beneficence requires him to practise vandalism,
cruelty and homicide upon a vast scale and with
a refinement proportional to his knowledge and
inventiveness. It may well seem credulous to
find in this anything more than a fatal madness
by which man is hastened to his doom.

But there is just one angle from which it may
be possible to discern some method in this madness. We must learn to regard war, not as an
isolated phenomenon, but as merely the most
aggravated and the most impressive instance of
the universal moral situation. This fundamental
predicament of life, which gives rise to all moral
perplexities, is the *conflict of interests.* When
war is viewed in this light, we may then see in
justifiable war a special application of the most
general of all ethical principles, namely, the
principle of *discipline* or *provident restraint.* Given
the natural conflict of interests, this principle defines the only alternative to waste and mutual
destruction. It means simply that under actual

conditions the greatest abundance of life on the whole is to be secured only by a confining, pruning or uprooting of those special interests which imperil the stability and harmony of the whole.

When such restraint is not self-imposed, it must be imposed externally. The first lessons in restraint are doubtless learned from rivals and enemies who are governed by selfish purposes of their own. But the moral principle proper appears only when restraint is exercised with a provident purpose, that is, for the sake of the greater good that will result; as when a man refrains from excess for the sake of long life, or respects his neighbor's property for the sake of a general security and prosperity. Similarly a teacher or parent may restrain a wilful child, and a ruler a lawless subject, in the interest of all, including the individual so restrained. It is customary to question such motives, but the hypocrite would have no success, nor the cynic any claim to critical penetration, were these motives not so common as to establish the rule. As a matter of fact they are as solidly psychological as any fact regarding human nature.

Restraint, however exercised, is in its first effect negative and destructive. To set limits to an appetite, to bar the way to childish caprice, to forbid an act and call it crime, is in some degree to inflict pain and death, to destroy some living impulse. But it is none the less morally necessary. And it matters not whether the act of restraint be simple and unpremeditated or complex and calculated, involving hosts of men and all the complex mechanism of modern war. It is still possible, on the larger scale as on the smaller, that the act of restraint should be required by a larger purpose which is constructive and humane.

It is sometimes argued that an act of violence or coercion can have such a moral motive only when it is performed by a "neutral authority" who has nothing to gain or lose by the transaction. It is further argued that, since in the case of international disputes no such disinterested party exists, no use of violence or coercion can be justified. Persons who reason in this way must be supposed to believe in the miraculous origin of all kings and policemen. The forcible prevention of robbery must to their mind have become just, when and only when there suddenly appeared on the scene a special heaven-sent race of beings wearing blue coats and billies, and having no passions or property of their own.

As a matter of fact, however, robbers were first

put down by the robbed. Their suppression was justified not because those who suppressed them gained nothing by it (for they certainly did gain), but because that suppression was enacted in behalf of a general community good in which the interests of the robber and his kind were also counted. And whatever be the historical genesis of the state, whether paternity or plunder, this much is certain: that the functions of the state were at first, and have been in a measure ever since, exercised by men who have derived personal profit therefrom. The function of the state, its purpose of collective order, power and welfare, came into existence long ages before constitutions and charters of liberty made public office a public trust. Before men could learn to be governed well, they had to learn their first lessons of social restraint from whatever rude authorities were at hand.

Whence, then, are we to expect those international police to whom alone is to be intrusted the function of restraining predatory nations, and races filled with the lust of conquest? Are they to descend from above, clothed in uniform and wearing the badge of their office? It takes little historical sense to realize that we must first live through an age in which the principle of international restraint slowly gains acceptance, and is exercised by those nations who, primarily moved by an imminent danger to themselves, act also consciously and expressly in behalf of the larger good of mankind.

Let not any man say that the nation which feels itself to be actuated by such a double motive is insincere and hypocritical. This charge, if pressed home, would discredit all moral purpose whatsoever. Not only is it humanly possible that England, while saving herself, should at the same time wage war in behalf of the larger principles of freedom and international law; but all hope of a new order of things lies in the existence of just such a resolve so to protect and promote one's own interest as at the same time to conduce to a like safety and well-being in others.

We have thus, I believe, reached an understanding of the general principle by which war is justified. The righteous war is that waged in behalf of a higher order in which both of the warring parties and others of their rank may live together in peace. If one man restrains another he must ask no more for himself than he concedes to his enemy. This modicum which is consistent with a like privilege in others he calls his right, and the law eventually defines it and invents special agents for its protection.

A righteous civil war will be one in which a faction is restrained in behalf of a national good which is conceived to include both factions. Whether correct or mistaken in their judgment, such a purpose undoubtedly actuated the nobler spirits of both North and South in the American Civil War. To the South it was a war for independence, and to the North a war for the Union. That is to say, the moral motive in each consisted of a conscious provision for the equal good of the other. Each, while most immediately moved by its special interest, believed that interest to agree with the best interest of the other. Each had its plan for both, the South aiming at a relation of friendship between two autonomous neighbors, the North aiming at the common advantages of national coherence. Forces of destruction and ungovernable passions were let loose, and the most dreadful of tragedies was enacted. But the fact remains that such higher purposes did exist, and gave to the struggle its quality of idealism. Most living Americans, even those descended from the men of the South, now believe that the North was right in the sense of being guided by a sounder judgment.

That so furious a conflict should have divided men of equally high purpose, that even yet doubts should exist as to the merits of the dispute, is profoundly deplorable—deplorable in the sense that all human blindness and frailty is deplorable. But it was not to be avoided by either scepticism or inaction. It was then, as always, a question of controlling events according to one's lights, or being controlled *by* them. There is no guarantee against the possibility of error, and in judgments regarding political policy the margin of error is large. Even if such a guarantee were theoretically possible, events would not wait for one to find it. A man must act when emergencies arise and circumstances permit. The likelihood of error does not absolve him from the duty of making up his mind and acting accordingly. To be honestly mistaken is at least better than to be impotently non-committal. For an honest mistake is at least an experiment in policy and a lesson learned.

The forcible restraint of one individual by another, or of one faction by another, may thus be said to be justified when it is necessary to the establishment of a relationship which is tolerable to both. In an established civil order this relationship is enforced by agencies especially provided for the purpose. These agencies, with the

sentiment which enlivens them, and the custom
and opinion which confirm them, signify good of
a higher order than that of any individual or
special interest; not because they are different
in quality, but because they include *all* individual
and special goods and make provision for them.
In the state we all live and are strong, and if it
fall,

> "O, what a fall was there, my countrymen!
> Then I, and you, and all of us fell down."

Now let us suppose nation to be arrayed against
nation. The use of force will be justified so far as
it is necessary to establish a relation between
nations that shall at least provide for their security. A nation which defends itself against aggression is both saving itself and also contending
for the principle of nationality. It asks no more
for itself than it concedes to its opponent—the
privilege, namely, of existing and of administering
its own internal affairs. Such a defensive war
has then a double motive, the narrower motive
of national security and the higher motive of
general international security.

Even the narrower of these motives is a moral
motive for the individual. The state is for most
men the highest good which comes at all within

the range of their experience. It is incomparably
superior to the good with which in the daily round
of work and play they are mainly preoccupied.
It is often ignored, even by those persons of un-
selfish purpose who oppose war because it threatens to interrupt the work of social betterment.
Thus Mr. Philip Snowden, M.P., eloquently ex-
horts us to "realize that a beautiful school is a
grander sight than a battleship—a contented and
prosperous peasantry than great battalions." [1]
Nobody in his sober senses would deny it. But
let Mr. Snowden and his friends on their part
realize that his beautiful school and his prosperous
peasantry exist by the grace of a state which
owes its origin and its security to the vigilance
and energy of men who have valued it enough to
fight for it.

The security of the state means the security
of all the good things that exist within the state.
We in America are fond of being let alone. The
thought of war annoys us because life is so full of
good things that we hate to be interrupted. But
liberty and opportunity are the fruits of our national existence, and if we love them we would do
well to cherish that national existence in which

[1] From a speech delivered before the House of Commons on
"Dreadnoughts and Dividends," on March 18, 1914.

they are rooted. Fighting men as a rule understand this better than peacemakers. The individual understands it better on the field of
battle than he does in the place where he earns
his living or in the place where he goes when he
is tired. It has become the custom to emphasize
man's savagery, and belittle or suspect his sentiments. We need to be reminded that the average soldier thinks and feels more generously
than the average civilian. We have come to
speak of patriotism as though it meant mere self-
assertion, and have forgotten that patriots are
individuals who, while collectively they may be
asserting themselves against the enemy, are individually denying themselves for their country.
And it is of this self-denying loyalty that they
are most keenly conscious. "The peace advocates," wrote Mr. E. L. Godkin in the days of
Gravelotte and Orleans, "are constantly talking
of the guilt of killing, while the combatants only
think, and will only think, of the nobleness of
dying."[1]

It is only in national emergencies that the
great majority of men realize that they enjoy
the benefits of national existence. Then only is

[1] From the article on "Peace" in his *Reflections and Comments*,
p. 3.

it realized that civic life is the fundamental condition of individual life, and that all forms of
economic and cultural activity are vitally de-
pendent on it. The generation that has been
born in this country since the Civil War has
never had to make sacrifices for the state, and
has never been brought to such a realization.
We have taken too much for granted. Like
spoiled children, we have assumed that the staple
good of national security was provided by the
bounty of nature, and have irritably clamored for
the sweetmeats of wealth and higher education.
I do not mean to suggest that any people should
be satisfied with the minimum, but that we
should clearly understand that human goods
must follow in a certain order, and that the super-
structure rests upon the foundation.

But while the good of the state is greater than
that of any individual or special interest, because
it contains all of these and nourishes them, how
shall it be measured against the good of that
other state against which it is arrayed in war?
How is it possible to justify patriotism when it
makes war on patriotism? Is the state worth
fighting for, when it means that there is another
state which one is fighting against? Again we
must apply our principle, that force is justifiable

only when used in the interest of both parties, or in behalf of some higher form of association that is inclusive of both. A just defensive war must therefore be actuated by a higher principle even than that of patriotism. While it is waged primarily on behalf of the great common good of national existence, there must be at the same time a due acknowledgment of the enemy's equal right. The enemy on his part is deserving of forcible restraint only in so far as through his arrogance he prevents or threatens a relationship in which there is room for him as well. War upon such an enemy, like all righteous war, is war upon lawlessness. Although its first effect is destructive, it is provident and constructive in its ulterior effect.

With this principle in mind we may now take a further step and justify offensive war, when undertaken in the interest of an international system or league of humanity. For a century or more this greater cause has stirred the imaginations of men, and it has gradually been adopted as a norm for the criticism of international policy. There is now no serious doubt in liberal and earnest minds of the superiority of this cause to the narrower claims of nationality. How shall nations be so adjusted as to help and not hurt one another?

How shall commerce and cultural intercourse be promoted, and dangerous friction and rivalry be removed? How shall the threat of war be so far reduced that nations can direct their energies and resources internally to the improvement of the lot of the unprivileged and disqualified majority? In theory the answer is as obvious as it is trite: by establishing among nations some greater unit of civic life, some system of international law and equity, with agencies for its application and enforcement.

But how shall we go forward to this end? Not by abandoning what has already been achieved, the integrity of the nation. For what we seek is something greater than nationality, not something less. Not by sitting idly by and allowing events to roll over us. Not by awaiting the sudden appearance on earth of some heaven-sent umpire who shall box our ears and set us about our business. This much seems clear: that this end, if it is to be achieved at all, must be achieved by the greatest forces that man has now at his disposal. Nations and leagues of nations must assume the functions of international control. Their very strength, so terrible in destruction, must be directed to the larger end of construction. Just as the order-loving individual had first to enact the law for himself and in his own behalf, so the more enlightened and more liberal nations must take upon themselves the functions of international justice. One such nation, or an alliance of such nations, will be its first rude organ. Such an organ will necessarily be governed in part by the nearer motive of party interest, but this need not prevent the genuine existence of the higher motive as well. And just as the evolution of democracy means the gradual purification of the governmental motive, the purging of it from admixture with personal, dynastic and class interests, so we may expect to witness on the larger scale the gradual evolution of some similarly disinterested agency that shall represent the good of all mankind.

It is commonly and truly said that the present war is the most terrible in history. We have, I believe, been too quick to see in this a reason for despair. Wars become terrible in proportion to the strength of the warring parties, in numbers, organization and science. But what of this strength? Shall we count *it* no achievement? A war between Italy and Austria is more terrible than a war between Venice and Genoa, but only because Venice and Genoa have learned to live in peace and have achieved the strength of union and co-operation. We are witnessing to-day, not a mere war between nations, but the more awful collision between alliances of nations. The horror of the catastrophe should not blind us to the fact that France and England, for example, have learned that each has more to gain from the other's prosperity than from its decay, and that their differences are negligible when compared with their common interests. Together they possess strength of a higher order, terrible in war, but proportionally beneficent in peace. The evolution of human solidarity and organization has brought us to the stage of great international alliances.

It is thus in keeping with the record of human progress that the last war should be the worst— and the worst the last. For the only human force more terrible than a league of some nations is the league of all nations, the league of man. The same motive that has led to the one will lead to the other—the desire, namely, to avoid the loss and weakness of conflict, and to attain the incomparable advantages of co-operative life. This last alliance will then have no human adversary left, but may devote its supreme power to perfecting the lot of the individual, and scotching the devil of reaction.

The goods that are worth fighting for are first of all *existent* goods, embodied in the life of man.

Such goods are created by physical forces, may be destroyed by physical forces, and may require to be defended by physical forces. They are *worth* fighting for when they are greater goods than those which have to be fought against. Civil law is worth fighting for, against the lawless individual. National integrity is worth fighting for, against disruptive factions or unscrupulous rivals. The general good of mankind is worth fighting for, against the narrower purpose of national aggrandizement. These greater goods are worth fighting *for;* nothing is really worth fighting *against.* It therefore behooves every highspirited individual or nation to be both strong and purposeful. Strength without high purpose is soulless and brutal; purpose without strength is unreal and impotent.

We in America cannot, it is true, afford to build armies and navies from sheer bravado. Our strength must be consecrated to the best that the most enlightened reason and the most sensitive conscience can discern. But, on the other hand, we cannot afford to cherish any ideal whatsoever unless at the same time we are willing to put forth the effort that is commensurate with its realization. The corrective of militarism is not complacency and neglect, but a humane purpose; and the corrective of pacifism is not a lapse into barbarism, but the acquiring of sufficient might and resolution to do the work which a humane purpose requires.

VII

NON-RESISTANCE AND THE PRESENT WAR

MR. BERTRAND RUSSELL, of Trinity College, Cambridge, is probably the most eminent of the small group of Englishmen who have openly advocated non-resistance as a present policy. His recent articles, published in this country, are admirable for their detachment and humanity; they might well serve as a model for the philosophical discussion of the great issues that are now hanging in the balance. And since non-resistance is not likely to find a more able protagonist than Mr. Russell, I have selected one of his articles, entitled "The Ethics of War,"[1] as an instance by which to judge the merits of that principle.

Although I disagree with almost every specific opinion which this article contains, let me first express my agreement with the *general* and underlying opinion that "the way of mercy is the way of happiness for all." This opinion is abundantly verified by human experience, past and

[1] *International Journal of Ethics*, January, 1915.

present, and is rapidly coming to be a common premise from which all philosophically minded persons argue. War in itself is an unmitigated calamity. It is not to be praised, but denounced; it is not even to be tolerated and idealized as a natural necessity, but is rather to be hunted to its sources and eradicated like a curable disorder. Granting this, what is the reasonable attitude toward the present war and toward its principal actors? It is here that Mr. Russell seems to me to be mistaken in his facts and in his inferences.

There is in this country and at least to some extent among the Allied Powers, a disposition to take international treaties and conventions seriously, and to condemn as "lawless" a nation that violates them. Mr. Russell regards this disposition as groundless because treaties are in practise "only observed when it is convenient to do so." They lack the sanction which enforces law, and serve only "to afford the sort of pretext which is considered respectable for engaging in war with another Power." Now I am willing to assume for the sake of the argument the doubtful thesis that nations do in practise universally disregard treaties at the dictation of selfish expediency. There remains the important fact, conceded by Mr. Russell, that such action is judged to be disreputable and "unscrupulous." How is that judgment, which already impels governments to seek a "pretext," to be so strengthened as to act as a deterrent?

The analogy of law, to which the pacifist appeals, would suggest a resort to force. But the enforcement of international law predicates an international organization resolved to substitute arbitration for war. How is such an international organization to be brought about? Only, it would appear, by the cultivation of opinion and habit. In short, before the present sentiment for the observance of international law shall be convertible into a sanction, it must be strengthened and attain to something like unanimity. To this end it is important that no breach of such conventions as are already in existence should be condoned. It is not by a passive admission of past and present lawlessness, but by a counsel of perfection and a stern condemnation of the common fault, that usage is to be improved. A cynical violation of treaties should to-day be denounced with a severity exceeding any judgment in the past, so that to-morrow this thing may become so damnable that no government shall dare to be found guilty.

The disputes of private citizens are not commonly settled, as Mr. Russell asserts, "by the force of the police," but by legal process resting on habit and intelligence. The police do not so much enforce law as prevent its *occasional* infraction. The great majority of persons, and all persons for the greater part of their lives, are "law-abiding."[1] If international law is to be similarly sanctioned, its observance must likewise rest on habit and intelligence. Nations must become generally law-abiding, before any international police can undertake to constrain law-breaking nations. "If the facts were understood," says Mr. Russell, "wars amongst civilized nations would cease, owing to their inherent absurdity." How is such a general understanding to be brought about, and how is the reasonable practise to become the normal practise? Only, it seems to me, by an unflagging effort to promote every instrument, such as international law, treaties, courts of arbitration,

[1] Mr. Russell, on the other hand, evidently agrees with the view of Mr. Strachey as quoted by Mr. Graham Wallas: "Why do men have recourse to a Court of Law in private quarrels . . . ? Because they are forced to do so and are allowed to use no other arbitrament." To this Mr. Wallas replies: "But, as a matter of historical fact, the irresistible force by which men are now compelled to resort to the law-courts in their private quarrels is the result of custom arising from thousands of free decisions to do so." —*The Great Society*, p. 169.

that provides a substitute for the absurdity of war, and by the emphatic and unambiguous *censure* of every act that destroys these instrumentalities or renders them ineffective.

To many minds it doubtless seems paradoxical to war for the sake of peace. It is precisely as paradoxical, no more and no less, as it is to labor for the sake of rest, or to make sacrifices in order that one may live more abundantly. Indeed I am inclined to go so far as to say that the one cause for which one may properly make war is the cause of peace. To be willing to fight for a thing simply means to be unwilling to give it up, however seriously it may be threatened. The one thing that is certainly worth the price of war is peace. This is simply because war means the destruction, and peace the security, of all human values.

The only justification of destruction is the hope of safety and preservation. This holds, whatever be one's values, provided only that they be human and earthly values. There is only one philosophy of non-resistance that can be justified, and that is other-worldliness. If no value attaches to the things of this world, then there is no motive for resistance; although in that case it is equally indifferent whether one resists or not, since the enemy's life is worth no more than one's own. The moment any human achievement of body, mind or character is taken to be good, then war for its preservation is in principle justified. Even though humility be the supreme good, then one should resist the aggression of an enemy who threatens to destroy one's life before one has cultivated that virtue, or proposes after the extermination of the humble to spread a propaganda of pride.

But Mr. Russell bases his claims for non-resistance on no such philosophy of renunciation. It is evident that he holds life, happiness, intellectual contemplation, self-government, and many other things to be good. He suggests nothing better worth struggling for than these characteristic benefits of the secular civilized life. He would propose to secure these things by peaceful means, but he must, of course, add, "if possible." What, then, if some enemy determines to destroy these things, and *begins* to destroy them? Suppose that enemy to be prompted by the motive of destruction. There are then only two alternatives: To yield, with the expectation that these good things will be destroyed, or to resist in the hope that they may be preserved, albeit at great cost and in diminished measure. In the former

case one's action cannot be justified at all because one can expect no good from it. One cannot even hope to avoid evil, because it may be
the determination of the enemy to perpetrate
that which one holds to be evil. The latter course
is then the only course that will be dictated by
love of good.

To try out this principle of non-resistance one
must imagine the greatest conceivable good to
be attacked with a deliberate intent to destroy
it; or the greatest conceivable evil to be threatened with a deliberate and implacable intent
to perpetrate it. One must suppose the success of the enemy to be probable if he is
not resisted, and doubtful or capable of being
retarded, if he is resisted. To test the principle
rigorously one should conceive the good or evil
at stake in such terms as to arouse one's deepest
sentiments. It is life, or character, or social
welfare, or the soul's salvation that is attacked;
it is tyranny, or rape, or child-murder, or hell-
fire that is threatened. What, then, shall one
do? To yield, not to resist to the utmost, is to
abandon the best or permit the worst. There is
by definition no higher ground, either the promotion of good or the avoidance of evil, on which
such a course may be justified. It is true that in

any given case one's judgment may be in error. But this proves only that one should be sure that one's fears are well grounded, that it is a genuine good or evil that is at stake, and that one's enemy is really one's enemy. This argues for the need of light. But it does not in the least argue against the principle of defensive warfare.

So much for the principle. Let us consider the author's applications. "The Duchy of Luxemburg, which was not in a position to offer resistance, has escaped the fate of the other regions occupied by hostile troops."[1] I am willing to waive the doubtful considerations of "honor" and "prestige," and stake the argument altogether on other considerations. First, Luxemburg through non-resistance has decreased the respect for the independence of small nations in general, and for her own independence in particular. Secondly, though she may have escaped the fate of the other regions occupied by hostile

[1] *Op. cit.*, p. 139. Mr. Russell does not present evidence that this is the case. The New York *Times* for February 23, 1915, published the following extract from a letter written from Luxemburg: "I do not believe that the Belgians can hate the Germans as strongly as the people of this little duchy. Their country is not laid low by cannon-fire, neither were they butchered by the Germans, and yet they are not better off than the inhabitants of Belgium. Every able-bodied citizen is being compelled to serve the German army in one or other form. . . . The laboring classes have lost their occupations, while the well-to-do cannot point to anything and say, 'This is mine.'"

troops *thus far*, it is as well to remember that the war is not yet over. If the tide turns, the inhabitants of this duchy may yet be visited with all the horrors of war, with no friend on either side, and incapable of protecting themselves. Thirdly, if Germany wins, Luxemburg becomes, as she is virtually now, a German dependency. If Germany loses, Luxemburg has small claim for the recognition of her sovereignty even from those who are in this war the champions of the smaller states, on the principle that those deserve political autonomy who care enough for it to defend it. Finally, Luxemburg does not in any case offer an analogy from which to argue for the non-resistance of Belgium or England, because she "was not in a position to offer resistance," and therefore was under no such recognized obligation to defend her neutrality as was the case of Belgium.

But Mr. Russell is evidently willing to contemplate, as preferable to warlike resistance, even loss of political independence. He evidently believes that what is valuable in national life may be preserved even though one put oneself utterly at the disposal of the enemy. Here again I prefer to waive the more doubtful matters. Whether humiliating submission to alien arrogance, accompanied by a vivid memory of lost freedom, would be a tolerable form of existence, I will not attempt to argue—I should fear that I might lapse into an expression of feeling. Most men would, I think, prefer to die; and they would be entitled to the choice. But Mr. Russell proposes somehow to combine with non-resistance "English civilization, the English language, English manufactures," and English constitutionalism or democracy; all this, though the English navy were sunk and London occupied by the Prussians!

Now what can Mr. Russell mean? He knows better than I that not only manufactures, but bare existence in England depends on commerce. They depend not only on the actual freedom of the sea, but on the *guarantee* of that freedom. He knows that if the Prussians occupied London and it suited their purpose they could undertake the suppression of the English language as they have undertaken the suppression of the Polish language. He knows that, should the German monarchy fear the effect of the example of English democracy, it would have a strong motive for emulating the policy of the "Holy Alliance" of 1815. Having the motive, there is on the principle of non-resistance not the least reason why Germany should not accomplish these things.

Mr. Russell thinks that England may nevertheless be saved from oppression by "public opinion in Germany," which is somehow suddenly to be inspired with magnanimity by the spectacle of the voluntary submission of its rival. Germany's treatment of a non-resistant China would afford small encouragement for this desperate hope, even were it not a general fact that arrogance is only inflated and encouraged by submission. History abounds in examples of this. One need only cite the habitual insolence of the European races toward non-resistant or obsequious Jews.

The last remaining vestige of hope would then be based on Mr. Russell's contention that England herself has not found it possible to refuse self-government to her colonies. But England has found it necessary or politic to concede self-government to her *colonies* because they were *English* colonies, composed of high-spirited men of English blood who could be counted upon sooner or later to assert their independence, and to make it respected if necessary by force. England has not found it necessary to grant self-government to conquered races. An England occupied by Prussians would not be a colony, but a conquered race. And by the express terms of a philosophy of non-resistance such an England would have lost its high spirit, and would have renounced forever any ultimate appeal to force.

Like the American neutral, Mr. Russell holds "that no single one of the combatants is justified in the present war." What he means is not perfectly clear. That no nation whatsoever has clean hands and an unblemished record is doubtless true. But at least two of the warring nations, Servia and Belgium, were wantonly attacked. It is now generally admitted that Austria's ultimatum to Servia was intended to provoke war in order that Servia might be "chastised." Belgium was deliberately sacrificed to Germany's military convenience. So far as these nations are concerned, there was no alternative to war save non-resistance. Both of these nations belong to the side of the Allies. The other allied nations were at least in part moved by a desire to save these two smaller nations from subjection. They may be said, therefore, to be fighting for the principle of national security, and for the principle of adjudicating international disputes by conference, agreement and treaty. They were or are now doubtless actuated by other and less commendable motives. But that does not in the least annul their justification on the first ground. For a man may rightly save a weak neighbor from assault, even though the assailant be one's private enemy, and even though his punishment afford one private satisfaction or advantage.

Even were one to grant that Russia and France should have permitted the subjection of Servia by Austria, and that England should have permitted the subjection of Belgium by Germany, there remains an independent and much less debatable question. Which of the warring parties is most deserving of censure, and whose victory is more desirable? In other words, whom should one's moral judgment most severely condemn, and what outcome would be most conducive to the general good? This is a question which no lover of mankind, however detached and dispassionate, can ignore. The present war is an event of prodigious human significance, and its consequences will be lasting and far-reaching. If there be any just decision or verdict in these matters, it is important to reach it, lest one lapse into helpless and confused passivity, and play no part now that the hour of trial has come. There is a wide-spread conviction among those who have observed the war at some distance from the heat of action that Germany and Austria are chiefly culpable and that their defeat is desirable. It seems probable, more from what Mr. Russell has omitted to say than from what he has said, that he does not share that conviction. His independence and honesty of opinion are to be respected. But I believe his opinion to be mistaken.

Mr. Russell himself acknowledges that "democracy in the western nations would suffer from the victory of Germany." He protests, however, that democracy can never be "imposed" on Germany; overlooking the fact that a decline of Prussian military prestige would not only remove a threat that seriously retards the natural growth of democracy in England and France, but might put new heart into the millions of German Social-Democrats who (contrary to Mr. Russell's assertion) do not enjoy "the form of government which they desire."

Nothing that has developed during the last year of the war, and nothing that Mr. Russell has said, has tended to disprove the verdict that Germany and Austria are the principal offenders on whom may justly be visited whatever penalty be appropriate to the crime of war. The paramount fact is that one of these Powers, abetted by the other, first made war. Germany, at least thus far, has practised war least humanely, has done least to mitigate its horrors, and has shown least respect for the conventions which have been intended to regulate and limit war. The dominant party in Germany, the Prussian military caste, most perfectly embodies the aggrandizing and arrogant spirit of aggressive war, and constitutes the greatest obstacle in the way of the achievement of future and perpetual peace.

If these judgments be well founded it is essential that they should be made and that they should not readily be forgotten. They may only too easily be confused by an overscrupulous regard for the guilt of the less guilty. There is a curious inversion of emphasis in Mr. Russell's article. It is not impossible that a distrust of vulgar opinion should lead a nicely analytical and cautiously reflective mind to exaggerate whatever is contrary to the general prejudice. It may even lead one to dwell at length upon the immoderate indignation of the victim, while the fury of the assailant rages unrebuked. It is doubtless the principal task of the philosopher to offset the bias of the multitude and resist the current that sweeps by him. But it sometimes happens that the common opinion is correct, and that even such blind passions as patriotism and righteous indignation will be found working for the general good.

VIII

WHO IS RESPONSIBLE?

A^T a time like the present there is no maxim
in the whole store of moral truisms that is
not apt. For war appears to be nothing less
than a demoralizing of man, a fit of madness in
which riotously, even exultingly, he throws away
all the advantage he has laboriously won against
the inertia and drag of nature. As though seized
with a sort of morbid exhibitionism, he denudes
himself of the garment of civilization and shame-
lessly exposes what he once thought bestial and
degraded. Deceiving himself by narrow and per-
verted loyalties, and confirmed by the unison of
collective passion, he launches himself upon a
course of violence, deceit, robbery, arson, murder,
profligacy, cruelty, lawlessness and impiety—so
that war seems scarcely other than a name for
the aggregate of all wicked things.

This is incontestable. But save as a purge for
the writer himself there is little virtue in saying
it, because it needs so little arguing, and because,

as with most sermonizing, the sinners are not in
church.   The cure of the present war is not to be
effected by gentle remonstrance.   Then why all
this talk ?   Why does every man burn to say something, if only to his neighbor over the back fence?
It is because we have reflected that what has
happened once may happen again, and that the
horrid menace of war must be taken to heart.
Mankind is liable and even predisposed to contract the disease and perish of it.   We are rightly
stirred to seek measures of prevention; not for
our own selves merely, but because civilization
itself is worth so little while it is threatened with
sudden and ruinous depreciation.   If any cause of
war can be unmistakably identified and labelled
"Danger!" then something, be it ever so little,
has been contributed to the safety of mankind.
To know a cause prepares the way for its control, and to control the cause is to control the
effect.

But first of all it is necessary to believe and to
believe resolutely and unyieldingly that war has
causes which may be identified and controlled.
To doubt this is as though medical science should
disbelieve in the possibility of curing disease.
Whoever says that the present war or any war
is inevitable, should be rebuked as the unwitting

accomplice of the powers of darkness. For in weakening the intent and power to control the disaster he is helping to bring it about. He who regards any event as inevitable is himself one of its causes. This is the obvious but neglected truth that I want here to proclaim. War does not *happen to* mankind, but is *committed by* mankind. It is as much within his control as are any of his works, and to fall away from this belief into a weak and hopeless acquiescence, is to lose that high purpose from which all great human achievements must spring.

By a curious perversion of an obscure half-truth common sense has come to regard the psychological, or the "merely" psychological, as unreal. Christian Science relies upon this vulgar prejudice to convince people that to identify disease with error is the same as to deny it altogether. The worldly wise have had a good deal of fun over President Wilson's declaration that the ante-bellum business depression was largely psychological. Assuming that this was the same as to say that there wasn't any business depression, the rustic or curbstone wit had only to point to some recent failure, and loutish laughter rang loud at poor Mr. Wilson's expense. So one hesitates to say that war is largely psychological,

lest some keen observer point to the record of
death and destruction, and ask triumphantly:
"Are these, too, psychological?"

And yet it is instantly evident that everything
whatsoever with which man has to do is in so
far a matter of human nature, that is to say, of
psychology. I am assuming that we are talking
not of events like the return of a comet, but of
events like wars in which human agency is involved. Wars are due not to the operation of
mechanical laws of the astronomical sort, but to
the passions, purposes, decisions and volitions
of men. They are due, in short, to the human
mind, as this operates individually and collectively.

That there are enormous differences in the
causal power exerted by different minds, depending on their place of vantage in the social
system, is, of course, true. Most men merely
echo the prevailing opinion or swell the general
tide of passion. Even so, such men in the aggregate give to opinion its tendency to prevail, and
to passion its tidal and overwhelming power.
But the contribution of a single member of the
mass is not comparable with that of an individual
who occupies a place of prominence or authority.
Such a mind operates at a source, coloring all that

springs from it, or at a crucial point where every slight deflection is enormously magnified in the consequence. From such minds come the models of opinion, the first breaks in the self-control that dams the flood of passion, or the decisions and acts which suddenly create new situations and upset the delicate equilibrium of peace. The causes of any war are far too complex for exhaustive analysis. The historians have not yet satisfactorily explained the first war, and we shall not live to see the explanation of this last. But so much is certain, that wars are due to the forces which animate and govern the human mind.

Now to return to our truism, that to expect war is to be a contributory cause of it. To expect a thing is in a way to dispose one's mind to it; and if it be the sort of thing, like war, that is a product of the mind, it will therefore be affected —if not directly and considerably, then at least indirectly and slightly. Only be it remembered that causes that severally are slight may cumulatively be decisive. To expect a thing is usually to relax or abandon efforts to prevent it. The expectation of failure weakens the effort to succeed, and in so far makes way for failure. Similarly, to expect a war inclines one to be half-hearted or to lose heart altogether in one's efforts to keep the peace.

In the case of war a peculiar social phenomenon aggravates this negative effect of unbelief, and exerts a positive influence as well. To disbelieve in the friendly intentions of another, to regard him as an enemy, is to encourage in him whatever incipient hostility his breast may harbor. The hostility thus evoked will seem to justify the very suspicion that evoked it. This suspicion, in turn, now renewed and intensified, will react again upon its object until, passion thus feeding on itself, what was at the outset only a passing attitude of faint distrust has become a violent and deep-rooted hate. Every one has witnessed this phenomenon in spitting cats and growling dogs, or in the growth of his own personal enmities. To understand the part such causes play in war one has only to multiply these familiar effects by the factors of contagion and social intensification.

But expectation involves more than lapse of prevention. Ordinarily it involves something more positive still, that we call "preparation for the inevitable." And to prepare for a thing in that spirit is, of course, to facilitate it. If you are resigned to an event, then you have created conditions favorable to its occurrence. To be ready for war means that any new event tending to war will find other necessary factors already present, so that what is in itself a cause of slight weight may be a last straw. The materials, the organization, the policies, even the explanations and apologies are at hand. The normal inhibitions against violence are largely removed. To be ready for war is to be, as we say, "used to the idea." There are a thousand ways in which preparation for war, itself the consequence of expecting it, may in turn literally pave the way for it, or pass over by almost insensible gradations into the act of war itself.

The question of preparedness is thus, like most questions of policy, less simple than immediately appears. Since war may always be forced by the threat of something worse, prudence and a decent sense of responsibility compel even a peace-loving nation like the United States to be prepared for that emergency. Furthermore, there are times and circumstances like the present, in which war is a very live possibility. It may be a war of defense; it may be a war on war-makers in the interest of peace. It is necessary, then, to prepare for the *contingency* of war, without regarding it as inevitable. Lest even this readiness should dispose the mind to accept war as a fatality, it is necessary at the same time to labor eagerly and hopefully for peace. There is a vast difference between being resigned to failure and being prepared for failure, and the difference is made by the determination to succeed. It is possible to prepare for war without being resigned to it, provided one struggles with conviction to achieve an honorable peace.

So much for our generalizations. Let us fit the cap. Many who have recently undertaken publicly to justify Germany have betrayed on their own part, and have attributed to Germany herself, a belief that the present war was inevitable. There is one infallible sign of fatalism. Believing as they do that an event is inevitable and that individuals like themselves are both impotent to prevent it and free from responsibility for it, all fatalists attribute the event to extra-individual causes, to abstractions and fictions which they suppose to operate somehow, despite individuals.

Most of us can remember that it was not we ourselves, but "destiny" that annexed the Philippine Islands. We now find the minds of German apologists confused with a like superstition. Avoiding the history of the crucial decisions and actions of individuals, like Count Berchtold and

Emperor William, they tell us that the war is due to the "racial ambition" of the Slav, to the French sentiment of "revanche," and to British "commercial jealousy." Owing to the operation of these forces the war was "bound to come"; these were its great "underlying causes."

Now, is this cant or only pedantry? Is it mere talk by which to mask ambition, or is it a sincere wrong-headed abstractionism tinged with sentimentality? Perhaps it is both. When the motives of a nation are in question it is safer to adopt the more complex rather than the simpler theory. In any case the causes invoked, taken as impersonal forces, are sheer nonentities; they cannot cause war for the simple reason that except as particular motives in concrete individuals they do not cause at all.

There are Slavs, no doubt, who cherish dreams of racial unity and aggrandizement, as there are Servian and Russian politicians who contrive ways of realizing such dreams. But these are individuals governed by countless other motives as well, limited by opportunity, liable to change, and in some measure open to reason. There are vindictive Frenchmen and jealous Englishmen, no doubt; but the individual minds that harbor these passions are moved also by other impulses, and are capable, judging by the history of the last decade, of controlling their passions.

Granting that, it is impossible to deny that these passions might subside and disappear altogether. If a war can be postponed a day or an hour, no man can deny the possibility of preventing it altogether. Woe to the man who takes the last irretrievable step that cuts off that possibility forever. For he has committed the act of war; aided and abetted by all who have confused his mind and blinded him to his crucial and decisive responsibility. To single out some one sentiment from the rest, to abstract it from the individual minds that entertain it and from the circumstances that limit and change it, to invest it with a power to operate *in vacuo* and with superhuman power like an evil spirit, is both a silly superstition and, in the practical aspect, a culpable abandonment of moral effort.

Apparently the "if there be war" was to the German authorities so vivid a possibility, so overwhelming a probability, that they were unwilling to risk any military advantage whatsoever in the interest of a thing so chimerical as peace. If Germany had been willing to lose the advantage of swifter mobilization by postponing the outbreak of war until Russia was mobilized,

there is every reason to believe that the war
would not have broken out at all. It is fairly
evident that you cannot keep the peace by insisting upon an arrangement such that you would
enjoy every initial advantage if there should be
war. There results a manœuvring for position
that is already a beginning of war. It is true·
that every nation is in a measure guilty. For
years Europe has been so zealously engaged in
a hypothetical war as to make the transition to
real war an easy and natural one. But it can
scarcely be denied that efforts to reduce arma-
ments and establish peace upon a permanent
basis have met with least encouragement in Germany, and this owing not so much to German
militarism as to German scepticism.

The German loves peace, but doesn't believe
in it; he hates war, but resigns himself to it as
inevitable. The Yellow Peril or the Slav Peril
is forcing it upon him, and thrusting the sword
into his reluctant hands. With admirable resolution and skill he makes ready to meet these
fantastic perils, and lo, by his very readiness he
has made them for the first time real. He has
himself brought the Japanese to Kiaochow and
the Russian to Königsberg.

If German explanations of the war have con-

firmed and aggravated the prejudice they were
designed to correct, it is because they fail to go
to the individual centres of human responsibility.
It is natural for Englishmen or Americans to
want to know *who* made the war, not *what* made
it. And this is not a mere habit of mind; it is
good history and sound psychology. In order to
cause events, the passions which move men and
societies must find expression in action. Before
they can do this they must undergo selection and
limitation, through their reciprocal interplay,
and through the various checks of habit, authority and reason. Eventually passion may pass
over into volition and overt action. But it is
during this transition from tendencies and potentialities to particular acts of particular individuals
that they are subject to control. The tendencies
and potentialities themselves, such as race hatred
or land hunger, are indeterminate as to their
effects. They may result in this or that, according to the turn they are given at the crisis of
action. The full absurdity of invoking them as
causes of war can be understood only when one
reflects that there always exist such causes of
war between all the peoples of the earth. They
are among the constant forces which human
policy must take account of, but they are not the

differential causes which actualize specific events, nor the instrumental causes with which these are controlled.

We do not explain the sinking of the *Titanic* by the law of gravitation. Ships do tend toward the bottom of the sea, as men tend to lie prone upon the earth; nevertheless many ships float and men do for a time stand erect and even rise into the air. In other words, there are other forces besides gravitation, and the physical history of man is due to the balance and regulation of these forces. There is jealousy, bitterness and suspicion enough between some Americans and some Japanese to provide abundant "underlying causes" for the outbreak of war. And should such a disaster be visited upon us no doubt these and other more remote generalizations would be invoked in order to obscure and excuse individual responsibility. But it will in fact be as unnecessary to-morrow as to-day, unless it be for the wanton recklessness, selfishness or stupidity of some individual who at a particular crisis allows these sentiments to break forth into hostile deeds. There are underlying causes for a brawl between every man and his neighbor, inasmuch as there are in every human heart impulses of self-aggrandizement and anger that would, if conditions were favorable and checks removed, drive each man at his neighbor's throat. But when such deeds of lawlessness occur we do not ascribe them to these impulses, but to the defects of will and reason by which they were let loose.

Human nature is warlike. True, but not conclusive. The Eskimos of Greenland and the African Pigmies, for example, are not at war. Then we must add that human nature, conditions being favorable, is also peaceful. And if we admit this, we must conclude that since man is capable of either, whether he be at war or at peace, is going to be determined not by these deeper and more constant capacities, but by the conditions that stimulate, evoke and facilitate them. These conditions may be controlled so that the peaceful possibilities are realized, and the warlike possibilities held in check or transmuted into their opposite. In this fact lies the hope of civilization.

IX

THE UNIVERSITY AND THE INDIVIDUAL

THE recent course of events has forced to the front an old and crucial issue. The need for economic and military preparedness, for a more vivid national consciousness, and for some comprehensive and synthetic treatment of acute social maladies, have steadily inclined opinion toward centralization and institutional control. But this trend appears to threaten that individual latitude and diversity which is the most cherished tradition among English and French speaking peoples. It behooves us, then, to seek for the tap-root of that individualism which we prize, in order to know on what its life and nourishment depend.

It has often been observed that what imperils individualism in these United States of America in this twentieth century is not institutional tyranny, but the unconscious and insidious tyranny which is exercised by the unorganized social mass. Here is a tyranny that is not only powerful, but capricious. It has not even the merit of consistency. And the individualism which it suppresses is the essential individualism. Institutional authority, however tyrannical, may at least be credited with suppressing that lawless self-seeking which borrows the honorable name of liberty, but which is in fact its most ancient enemy. The mass influence, on the other hand, is a menace to that self-possession, that capacity for private judgment which is the soul of all disciplined and constructive liberty.

Since tyranny of this sort is not imposed by institutional authority, it is futile to resist it merely by political means. It is not to be met directly either by curtailing the functions of the state or by enlarging the political activities of the individual. For it is primarily a question of how much *thinking* an individual is going to do for himself. The more a man thinks, the less is he imitative and suggestible. The problem, then, is to promote the practise of thinking. The problem is to be solved, if at all, by educational agencies, and these agencies must be directed to the end of cultivating theoretical capacity, or the gift of knowledge. For to create a knower is to create an individual who may, notwithstanding the pressure of the social mass, remain an individual.

This platitude becomes less insufferable when

one emphasizes the difference between knowledge and opinion, which everybody admits and which everybody ignores. That common sense is careless about this difference is proved by the fact that the term "knowledge" is perpetually employed where the terms "opinion," "information" or "belief" would be more correct. For most of us the first lesson in knowledge proper is geometry. We may remember, for example, the theorem that the sum of the interior angles of a triangle is equal to two right angles. We have all forgotten how the proof runs; but we can, perhaps, recover what happened to our minds in the course of it. When we came to the theorem we knew what we were going to prove. One might say carelessly that we already "knew" that the interior angles of a triangle were equal to two right angles. But that would be to overlook the immensely important difference between the state of mind before and after the understanding of the proof.

Before the proof we believed the proposition as hard as we did afterward. Our opinion was not changed. Nor did we get any new information. A surveyor who wished simply to *use* geometry, would have been as well off before. There are handy manuals of geometry for surveyors or navigators which contain only the theorems themselves without the proofs. But if we had simply learned from such a manual we would have failed altogether to experience just that flash of insight, that moment of illumination, when the proof is complete and one feels a comfortable glow in one's rational parts. I do not believe that there was ever a mind so benighted as not to experience a tiny bit of pleasure at just that moment when it can say: "I see!" If one were a cock this would be the time to crow. But whether it be joyous or not, this is the moment of *knowledge*.

In other words, to know, one must know *why*, or *on what grounds*. For every proposition that is true there is somewhere a "because," the evidence that proves it. To assert the proposition *in the light of the evidence for it*, is to know. The evidence is not always, or even usually, of the geometrical sort. The proof of a pudding, for example, is in the eating. I am not insisting that everything must be argued or reasoned about in order to be proved, but only that for every assertion that is true there is some kind of a proof, and that one does not "know" the assertion unless one's mind takes in the proof as well.

Now it is evident that if knowledge is to be

defined in this very exacting way, then there cannot be nearly so much of it in the world as is ordinarily supposed. If everybody were forbidden to say anything that he couldn't prove, a sudden hush would fall upon the world, and such events, for example, as an afternoon tea, or a debate in Congress, or the present essay would have to be stricken off the program altogether! If no one were allowed to use or act on any propositions that he couldn't prove, most of the business of life would have to be stopped, and very few things indeed would get done. No, I do not recommend that opinion, belief and information be abjured altogether, and that knowledge be put in their place. But, on the other hand, it does seem fairly apparent that somewhere, once in a while, there should be somebody that knows. Otherwise one does not see any way in which opinion, belief and information could be tested for truth, and have their trustworthiness guaranteed.

Theoretical capacity, then, means first of all the capacity to make truth, to reach sound conclusions, and to distinguish between well-grounded and ungrounded assertions. But it involves, furthermore, some comprehension of the limits of knowledge. The common failure to understand the limits of practical knowledge is a case in point. If I know that by combining with another man, *B*, I may crush out a third competitor, *C*, monopolize an industry, raise prices, and win a fortune, my knowledge may be well-grounded, based upon the incontestable evidence of experience. But there is also much that I do not know; for example, what effect such practises may have upon the industrial world at large, and what effect this effect in turn may have upon the health of the body politic or upon the general welfare of men. I do not even know what effect the winning of the fortune may have upon my own personal happiness, or the saving of my soul. If I act on the narrower knowledge as though it were all-comprehensive, I am guilty of the sort of ignorance which consists in ignoring how little, after all, I do know; and my practical wisdom may, because of its very cock-sureness or sense of certainty, turn out to be the most egregious folly. Or if, having learned a little science, say, for example, the theory of electrons, I straightway proceeded as though I lived in a world constituted wholly of electrons, and remained ignorant of moral or religious truths, I should be so lacking in sense of proportion as to imperil all my deeper interests. This is what is meant when it is said that "a little knowledge is a dangerous thing." A little knowledge is dangerous when it is mistaken for much.

It is important, then, to have the unknown charted on the map as well as the known. And it is scarcely less important to know the difference between certain knowledge and probable knowledge. It appears that the certainty of knowledge is in inverse proportion to its importance. Every one would agree, I think, that the biggest questions are those of politics and of religion. And yet here it is impossible to reach any conclusion at all comparable in certainty with the knowledge that "this book is on this table." Therefore we should learn so far as possible to regard prevailing opinions in the larger and more complex matters as subject to correction. If we do not, we simply cut ourselves off from the possibility of increased light where we are most in need of it.

Theoretical capacity is sustained, furthermore, by that primitive instinct of curiosity through which the pursuit of knowledge may be made to bring satisfaction of itself. It is an instinct which requires to be kept alive or reawakened, rather than an artificial interest which requires to be cultivated. There is no one who has not once felt this curiosity as a powerful impelling force. It is a matter of common observation and regret

that the sophisticated youth often shows less
eagerness of mind, less of that wondering, speculative impulse, than a small boy of seven. "No
sceptical philosopher," says Mr. Chesterton, "can
ask any questions that may not equally be asked
by a tired child on a hot afternoon. 'Am I a
boy? Why am I a boy? Why aren't I a chair?
What is a chair?' A child will sometimes ask
questions of this sort for two hours. And the
philosophers of Protestant Europe have asked
them for two hundred years." One who has met
with this sort of child will be surprised that Mr.
Chesterton should speak of the *child* as "tired."
Alas! it is the poor adult that is *tired*—perhaps
I should say bored, or at best patiently indulgent, because he has lost the hot interest, the ad-
venturous zeal from which these interrogations
spring. It isn't so much that the adult has
grown wiser, as that he has grown busier, and is
more dominated by habits, more broken to the
harness. He is already in the rut of practical
routine, and is annoyed at anything that suggests his ignorance and limitations.

Theoretical capacity, then, betokens the mind
which is emancipated from imitative or dogmatic
belief by a close regard for evidence and proof,
and which is emancipated from the narrowing

routine of "affairs" by that intellectual spontaneity with which every naïve mind is endowed. The quickened mind will complete its own emancipation. Thought loves generality and knows no bounds. It fixes upon the laws that abide, and neglects the local and the perishable. Its auxiliary and complement is the creative imagination—the one miracle that even science cannot deny, by which the mind may not only overcome time and space, but may also depart from the routine of perception and trace ideal connections and unities for the will to achieve.

The true individualism is this intellectual self-sufficiency, this capacity to do one's own thinking. Its substance is originality. It is not negative but creative. It is not lawlessness—a petulant assertion of impulse or private preference; but a deliverance from convention and the dead weight of vulgarity, to the end that the mind may freely judge and yield to the guidance of evidence and facts. It is that liberality of mind, that a large discourse, looking before and after, "that capability and Godlike reason," which is not given to "rust in us unused."

This is essentially an individual and not a social attribute. Whereas passion may be social, only an individual can think. We speak, properly, of an angry mob. The mob itself may be angry—and is a very different thing from, say, a thousand men each of whom is angry all by himself. Individualities melt and coalesce in the heat of passion, and the mob feels and acts as a unity. There is also such a thing as social conscience, or as common opinion, or as customary belief. Opinion and belief are states of mind that may assume a social form. But there is no such thing as a mob's making inferences or demonstrating theorems or criticising action. Society cannot know the sense of drawing a conclusion from premises or judging in the light of evidence. The weight of the social mass is perpetually tending to suppress these independent and solitary activities. In so far as the individual becomes absorbed in the mass he ceases to think, to criticise, and to know. The individual in detachment is the organ with which society has to do these things.

Shouting with the crowd is always the line of least resistance. But there never has been a time in the world's history in which blind social forces have been so strong. Through the increase of facilities for transportation and communication, and through the wide diffusion of the rudiments of education, all men are coming to form one great circle of gossip. The powerful forces that impel a man to go with his crowd, act with it, believe with it, feel with it, now operate over an enormous area, with a correspondingly irresistible power. The forces which thus bring men together do good or evil quite indifferently. It all depends on what direction they take. So far as they themselves are concerned, they may take any direction. Hence the unprecedented demand for a poise and independence that shall permit of insight and kindle beacon lights to show the way.

Where is that theoretical capacity which makes the free mind, to be cultivated? This is, I believe, the great and the unique opportunity of the university. Let the university dedicate itself to this one form of service, and make every concession which this service requires. Here is the crux of this much-disputed matter of academic liberty. Whatever restraints it may be necessary to impose elsewhere, the university should be the one community that tolerates eccentricity and conceit in the hope that once in a while they may be, as they often are, the marks of growing genius. Being normal, being a good average man, of the familiar and popular type, is certainly agreeable; but it should, in a university at least, be regarded as not deserving of special note or praise. Most men are normal, and many will inevitably be or become so, for the simple reason that we call normal what most men are or tend to become. Exceptionality, distinction is the thing, and to encourage it one must regard the freak or queer man not with hostility but with hopeful interest.

It is a great mistake to suppose that one institution like the university should be expected to do every good thing at once. We are grateful to Colonel Goethals for having built the Panama Canal; it would be unreasonable to withhold our praise until we have learned whether he is a good tennis-player or has a fine ear for music. If we can find a doctor who can cure our bodies, we do not ask him to save our souls. We do not charge him with impiety because he does not especially interest himself in the matter. Similarly, the university is not designed to be a nursery, reform school, Sunday-school, armory or social club. Other institutions are. Let each institution be judged by its success in its own field. Let the university be looked to as a school for intellectual leadership. If it does not do this work, criticise it—or, better still, help it. But

do not confuse the situation by asking it to protect the innocent, spread the true faith or stimulate good-fellowship. If it does these things, as
it no doubt will in a degree, so much the better; but they are not, in its case, the one thing
needful.

Above all, do not ask the university to be
merely useful. It would be much as though you
should ask Newton to be a mechanic or Raphael
a house painter. Keep the money-changer out
of the temple of knowledge. It is better that a
university should be a zoological garden of strange
beasts, or even a museum of antiquities, than
that it should become a mere corner of the mar-
ket-place. Disorder, impiety, iconoclasm are not
evils in a university. They are the by-products
and symptoms of its proper spirit and genius.
That which is evil, and evil unmitigated, is conservatism, traditionalism, worldliness, conven-
tionality, or the artificial prolongation of infancy.
Here the youthful intellect must be urged to play
with fire in order that it may receive its baptism.
The wholesome university type is the bold and
radical mind, that is not afraid to challenge the
existing order of things.

It is well that we should understand that a genuinely free mind will criticise both the economic

and the political establishments, as well as the prevailing religion—for which in these days we appear to feel less solicitude. It was once fondly supposed that a free mind could be confined to the circle of its own private thoughts, in order that institutions might go unscathed. This was the compromise adopted by the philosophers of the seventeenth century. Its impossibility is the lesson of the eighteenth century. Institutions lie in the path of the critical mind, which cannot ignore them without retreating. The radical mind, furthermore, perfects its service only through a criticism and rationalization of life. A university must not only protect the liberty of criticising economic institutions; it must cultivate the propensity to criticise them. For otherwise social progress is left to the spasmodic benevolence of those who possess, or to the hunger and resentment of those who want.

If the university to serve its end must be free from the control, or even the influence, of any economic establishment, it is no less necessary that it should be independent of political institutions or policies. Here is a point of contact between the life of the nation and the larger life of the race. It is necessary that a state should pursue a policy, and that a nation should have a special character, which at the same time distinguishes and narrows it. But national life needs to be kept sweet by open inlets from the common past, from different and complementary cultures, and from the great neutral world of the intellect and the imagination. The university is one of the greatest of these channels. Its place is not in the midst of the nation, but on the border where it may command what lies beyond.

If this be the true ideal of a university it is clear that it calls for a very special and generous kind of loyalty on the part of its benefactors, or on the part of the citizens who support it for the good of the community. If you would be the true friend or benefactor of a university give to it not in order that your opinions may prevail, but in order that truth may prevail. Serve it, not to promote your own ideas, but in order that there may *be* ideas. Rejoice that there is more in the world than you would ever have thought of yourself. Cheerfully tolerate, and even help, for the sake of the greater wisdom that may come of it in the end, opinions that you do not agree with. Encourage inquiry, criticism and knowledge even when you don't understand, and thereby prove that you have more confidence in man than you have in your own powers.

If this be the true ideal of a university it follows that its teachers should be primarily men of knowledge, men of trained critical, experimental and theoretical capacity. These men must be given the opportunity and the facilities for research. They must be admired for what they achieve in research, and not blamed for failure to achieve some other thing like popularity, or invention, or virtue, or personal beauty, which are not the particular ends to which they are called. And this spirit of research should be diffused among students, so that they may know how to value knowledge, or may know what they know and what they do not.

In other words, university teaching should be so conducted as to make every student acquainted with the way in which knowledge *is formed*, in order that he may know how far he may trust the prevailing ideas of his time. Those who devote themselves to the making of knowledge will necessarily be a small fraction of society, but all the more reason why good judgment, or the general capacity for criticism should be widely diffused. The very presence in an educational centre of men of intellectual originality will go far toward effecting such a result by example and contagious admiration. But it is also important that knowledge of all sorts should be so taught as to impart not only the conclusions, but also something of the method by which these conclusions are reached.   Every university student should be brought to the frontier where he may witness for himself the conversion of ignorance into knowledge, and where he may exercise himself in the art, even though he do no more than solve over again the problems which great investigators have already solved before him.

The great university teacher will at the same time quicken that native curiosity, that sheer inquisitiveness with which happily the mind is latently endowed.   The great teacher will be not he who fills, but he who opens, the minds of his students.   He will befriend the man who loves a problem and delights to solve it, in whom the intellect may enjoy itself at play; he will challenge and disturb that lost soul which seems to have no mind at all except a memory and a few prejudices. We hear much of the importance of having teachers who are vital, in touch with the world, or possessed of a magnetic personality.   But the teachers that have left the deepest impress upon me are those who somehow made me feel that to think and to discover and to know were glorious things in themselves; who never apologized for them or tried to justify them in terms of something else, but exhibited so sincere a devotion to them as to breed by contagion and example a like respect for them in others. The eager and devoted scholar, the man of powerful intellect and passionate devotion to truth, has the essentials of a great university teacher. The rest, whether he be handsome, amusing, facile, or worldly-wise, is comparatively unimportant.

Freedom and detachment of mind does not, as we have seen, imply that one shall occupy oneself with recondite or artificial topics. I am far from proposing that a university shall dedicate itself exclusively to the study of hyperspace, Indic philology, and the transcendental ego of apperception. These are proper enough objects of study, but they are not good illustrations of my meaning because they put the emphasis in the wrong place. It is not the subject of study that is to be detached from life, but the method and the mood of study. There is no better subject of study for the purposes I have in mind than life itself. I want simply to emphasize the difference between studying life and living it. The thing you study may be as practical as you please. One may study commerce, or politics, or the distribution of wealth, or human happiness, or any near and familiar thing. I want only to urge that it is the particular business of a university to promote a free, cool and profound study of these things: the sort of study which leads the mind to raise fundamental questions with a view to seizing on fundamental ideas, or in the hope of an occasional flash of insight by which one may see far beyond one's habitual horizon. A single swift and momentary vision thus granted may endure through life and make the difference for the balance of one's years between intellectual slavery and intellectual emancipation.

It is not that I disbelieve in education for service. It is for the sake of service that one must urge the university to promote intellectual independence and originality; for to do this is to render that peculiar service to which the university is dedicated and for which it is truly indispensable. And it is because every educated man with any strain of nobility in him is going out in the world to serve his fellows that he should take with him that which will increase and elevate his service. He must first learn to think for himself. But if he does, it will turn out in the end that he has been thinking for others. A man who does not think for himself does not think at all. Having that power, he may be qualified to enlighten and to lead, when otherwise he could do no more than follow blindly or exert himself at a task of which he does not know the meaning. I have not meant to encourage men to cut themselves off from their fellows and content themselves with their own study and meditation. There are a few men whose pre-eminent fitness for an intellectual life would justify them in taking this course. But they are very few. Most men must live out in the world. And there, out in the world, is where there is need not so much of what we call "men of the world" as of men of mind, men of the spirit. "It is easy in the world," says Emerson, "to live after the world's opinion; it is easy in solitude to live after our own; but the great man is he who in the midst of the crowd keeps with perfect sweetness the independence of solitude."

To care for truth itself, and to seek to beget in others, not the acceptance of one's own belief, but *the will to know*, points to tolerance as the great practical virtue which must characterize university life. An intolerant man will prefer to be surrounded by those who have opinions similar to his own, and will not care whether they think or not. A truly tolerant man will prefer to be surrounded by those who think, and will care comparatively little whether they agree with him or not. If any community is to be an intellectual centre, where intellectual work is done, where all men learn what intellectuality is, and where some may be expected to contract it themselves, there must be a love of truth itself, and an earnest desire that it shall prevail, which is stronger than the love of any single opinion. There must be a sort of intellectual high spirits, in which one loves a brave foe more than a craven follower. It is often supposed that being tolerant means having no conviction. Thus Robert Browning said: "There are those who believe something, and therefore will tolerate nothing; and, on the other hand, those who tolerate everything, because they believe nothing." But it is not impossible, nor even rare, among persons of genuine intellectual zeal both to have convictions and also to love in others that quality of mind that will express itself in contrary opinions.

I think that the noblest words which were ever said of university education were those said of Harvard by William James upon the occasion of his receiving the LL.D. degree in 1903.[1] He spoke as one who was in a certain sense an

[1] Published under the title of "The True Harvard," in *Memories and Studies*, pp. 348–355.

outsider at Harvard, for he had never been an undergraduate of the college; he had never sat in the cheering section at football games, he had not been a member of undergraduate clubs, and it is altogether probable that he had never participated in any form of collective college enthusiasm. He had no class to walk with in the commencement procession.   He did not seek to belittle these things because he had no part in them, but rather to describe another sort of loyalty which he and others like him felt no less deeply.   We may value our college, he virtually said, as we value our family, merely because it is ours, because we are bound to it by so many associations and traditions; or we may value it because of our pride in its greatness.   And he found the greatness of Harvard to lie, as he put it, in her being "a nursery for independent and lonely thinkers."   Speaking of those who, like himself, did not belong to the Harvard family in the narrower or more clannish sense, he said:

"They come from the remotest outskirts of our country, without introductions, without school affiliations; special students, scientific students, graduate students, poor students of the college, who make their living as they go.   They hover in the background on days when the crimson color is most in evidence, but they nevertheless are intoxicated and exultant with the nourishment they find here. . . . When they come to Harvard, it is not primarily because she is a club. It is because they have heard of her persistently atomistic constitution, of her tolerance of exceptionality and eccentricity, of her devotion to the principles of individual vocation and choice. . . . *Thoughts* are the precious seeds of which our universities should be the botanical gardens. Beware when God lets loose a thinker on the world—either Carlyle or Emerson said that—for all things then have to rearrange themselves. But the thinkers in their youth are almost always very lonely creatures. 'Alone the great sun rises and alone spring the great streams.' The university most worthy of rational admiration is that one in which your lonely thinker can feel himself least lonely, most positively furthered, and most richly fed."

There is no lover of Harvard who would not have Harvard be and remain deserving of such regard. There is no lover of any university who would not have his university cultivate and treasure this spirit, as the quintessence of liberal education. There is no true lover of America or of mankind who would not have this spirit diffused whether by the university or any other educational agency. It is the very savor of the salt of emancipation and liberty.

These are the qualities of mind in which true individualism is rooted: originality and independence, both in judgment and in imagination; a power to distinguish between knowledge and opinion, belief or information; a recognition of the limits and degrees of knowledge; a love of knowledge for its own sake; and a spirit of tolerant fellowship with all who love knowledge, whatever be the particular opinion that they hold. Only that which threatens these qualities of mind really threatens individualism. All else is external, of the body and the mechanism, not of the soul. So long as these qualities are fostered and diffused we need not fear whatever of disciplined will or of institutional organization may be necessary to carry forward the great designs of the national and collective life.

X

EDUCATION FOR FREEDOM

IT is unnecessary in these days to justify education. If there is any single idea about education that is now generally accepted, it is the idea
that education is useful to the individual and imperative for the community. We measure the
civilization of any nation or section by the test
of literacy, or by the educational facilities that
are open to its people. Wherever democratic
political ideals have come to prevail, it is a recognized duty of the state to provide education
freely for all, in at least the rudiments of knowledge. In our own country we have virtually
come to believe that mere poverty should not be
allowed to stand in the way of even a college or
university training for any individual who can
demonstrate his capacity and ambition. Wherever
high industrial or professional ideals prevail, the
importance of a prolonged and thorough training in engineering, law, or medicine is no longer
doubted. And wherever democratic social ideals
prevail, as notably in this country, it is clearly

recognized that education is the great equalizer, the means of compensating for the handicaps of birth or wealth, and of extending to all alike an opportunity of going as far in power, happiness and dignity as native capacity will permit.

So far we must all be in hearty agreement. It is because every one believes in education in at least these aspects that so great a number of flourishing institutions enjoy the support and loyalty of the state or of private friends and benefactors. I do not propose to prove these things that require no proof. I want to confine my efforts to the defense of an idea that is in some danger of being forgotten. I refer to the idea of what is sometimes called *liberal* education.

Whoever broadly surveys the history of education will see that, at the same time that education has been more widely diffused and has gained a stronger support from public opinion and from the state, it has come to mean something narrower than it once meant. The more clearly we have recognized that education is useful and necessary, the more narrowly have we come to *insist* upon its usefulness and necessity, and to be suspicious of any education the usefulness and necessity of which are not apparent. At the same time that the average man has come to be the friend and beneficiary of education, education has come to be the creature of the average man, and to reflect his characteristic standards and point of view. The danger is that, while everybody may become educated in a certain practical or vulgar sense, nobody will be educated in that other and less obvious sense in which the privileged class was once educated. There is danger, in short, that the very same forces of opinion that make it possible that everybody should be usefully educated should prevent anybody from being liberally educated.

Let me illustrate the tendency which I speak of by referring to the choice of studies in colleges where there is freedom of election. Even in the Eastern colleges with which I am most familiar, colleges such as Harvard and Princeton, where, whether rightly or wrongly, the older humanistic traditions are supposed to be especially strong, the most notable feature of student election is the large resort to economics. I have not the least inclination to disparage the subject. I do not even feel sure that the tendency will not turn out in the end to have been a wholesome one. But the significant thing and, I suspect, the ominous thing is the motive which leads the average student to make such a choice. It isn't that he is especially interested in the solution of economic problems. He may and often does find the subject dull and unilluminating. But he is usually going to be either a business man or a lawyer, and he has heard that economics has something to do with business and law. He doesn't know that this is the case or in the least understand the matter. Indeed, the authorities of the Harvard Law School explicitly discourage men from attempting in any way to anticipate their professional studies in college. But the average undergraduate I speak of has somehow got it into his head that the study of economics is a kind of preliminary study of business or law. And so he chooses it; which proves, at any rate, what he is looking for, what idea he has of a college education. He is supposing that the thing to do in college is to acquire the tools of some trade. Thus the college tends to acquire the spirit and tone of a trade-school.

Another indication of the same tendency is the fact, which I suppose to be generally true, that the part of our State universities that is least vigorous is usually the college, or department of liberal arts. If this is true, then it shows that those who support higher education, in this case the citizens of a State, believe in it chiefly as a means of training farmers, doctors, lawyers, teachers, stenographers, housekeepers, and engineers.

Now, it was once supposed that it was the most indispensable part of higher education to train, or rather to develop and cultivate, *men and women*. They were taught Latin, Greek, mathematics, history, literature, and philosophy, not with the idea that they could use these things in earning a living, but with the idea that they were good for the soul. Latin and Greek, for example, are not any less useful than they used to be. The difference is that we are now more anxious that everything should be useful. Once it was thought that a trained and well-stored mind, a free imagination, an acquaintance with the past and with its triumphs and its heroes, were somehow great and good things of themselves that went to make a full and noble life. Such a life was open only to the privileged few; but the important thing is that *it was regarded as a privilege*. Now that it may so much more easily be attained, it seems to have lost its value; and apprenticeship to a trade, once thought to be a disagreeable necessity, marks the limit of aspiration. Concerned to assert the dignity of labor, the modern world seems somehow to be assuming that there is nothing dignified in life except doing one's job or getting ready for it.

A student who called upon me the other day gave me a new and I should say ultramodern view of the value of the old humanistic studies. Having taken a chair near my desk, and cleared his throat, he launched the conversation by saying: "Professor, may I ask what you think of Emerson?" This may seem somewhat abrupt. But we who teach philosophy are not surprised at any question; at any rate, I answered the inquiring student as best I could. Whereupon he came back at me with more of the same kind. What did I think of Carlyle, of Tennyson? But there is a limit even to a philosopher's simple good faith. I must have betrayed some impatience or suspicion. Whereupon he finally confessed to me that he was at Harvard to learn the art of salesmanship. He was particularly interested in the sale of aluminum cooking utensils. Some one had told him that the thing to do was to engage your unsuspecting victim in general conversation on some theme remote from the object of your sinister design. In this way you gained his confidence. So he had come to Harvard to acquire conversational resources. It was evident that he believed in higher education. He could see the use of it. He could measure the value of poetry in terms of tangible frying-pans and tea-pots. He could even see a use in personal intercourse with his professors, since it might create a pretext for conversational practise.

So it appears that there is a chance for liberal studies even in a most severely utilitarian program! But do they need such a utilitarian justification? Are we to accept such a standard? Or have liberal studies a value peculiar to themselves which we are in danger of losing if liberal studies decay? I admit that I am a partisan in the matter. If all studies were compelled to prove their utility, philosophy would have to go by the board. I do not commend it to any one as a means of livelihood. But from a partisan you will at least get one side of the matter, and in this case the other side has advocates enough.

Now what is this unique and indispensable value that belongs to a liberal education? I should emphasize first the fact that liberal education brings us abreast of progress. If we are to accept the theory of Weismann and deny the inheritance of acquired characters, we must suppose that progress takes place, not through the line of descent, but through the continuity of tradition and environment. By heredity we transmit to our children approximately what our parents transmitted to us. Our children will stand at birth where we stood at birth, with the same native capacities and family traits. In the course of our lives we have acquired much—new ideas, new forms of skill, new habits of mind. But these our children will not inherit. Though we may, and in some respects certainly shall exceed the attainments of our parents, what we have gained cannot be transmitted simply by heredity.

Is there, then, no sense in which our children profit by what we have learned, and so enjoy advantages superior to those which belonged to us as the members of an earlier generation? Certainly, and here lies the point. Our children will be surrounded from birth onward by a different and more advanced environment. The most important part of that environment during the earlier and more plastic years will be ourselves, with the new things we have learned. If our children do not learn more, there is at least more to learn than there was when we were children. The parental type which is imitated by the children of to-day contains novelties which distinguish it from the grand-parental type which was imitated by the children of yesterday. But the family is by no means the only medium of imitation. Playmates, teachers, newspapers, employers, ministers, poets, all represent and typify the culture of to-day—and imprint its characteristic and novel form upon the growing and receptive minds of the younger generation.

We must, of course, get rid of the notion of generation succeeding generation, like the regiments of a marching army. Generations overlap. There are innumerably many of them alive together. There are those who are coming of age to-day, those who came of age yesterday, and those who will come of age to-morrow. If one cared to reckon in terms of hours, minutes and seconds, one would readily see that the number of different contemporary generations exceeds our power to count. Every individual is born into a world in which a certain type is growing to be old-fashioned, another dominates, and a third is regarded as advanced and radical. And there are indefinitely many degrees between. To-day horses are slightly old-fashioned, automobiles common and air-ships novel. This illustrates the present phase of civilization. A child that is just now most impressionable is having this phase impressed upon him. He will become used or assimilated to it, play his part in the invention and innovation which modify it, and live to see his children reared in a world in which horses are antiquated, automobiles old-fashioned, air-ships common, and I know not what, novel.

This, then, is the way that society moves. Strictly speaking, there is no such thing as a modern infant; merely as infant he does not represent one time any more than another. But there is such a thing as a modern world. And it is going to make a lot of difference to the hapless infant what world he is born into. The modern world stands ready to seize upon him and put the imprint of modernity upon him. And he will be, when the world gets through with him, a modern man. Progress is possible because the past holds over into the present in the shape of institutions, monuments, records, customs, and in the shape of an existing and slowly changing social type. An individual may profit by this progress, and thus enjoy an unearned increment, by virtue of growing up in the midst of these things, imitating them, learning them, entering into and becoming one with them. His advantage is not one of inborn capacity, but one of place in history.

But to return to our main point—the importance of liberal studies.   We may now say that
their importance lies first of all in their *enabling
an individual to enjoy to the full all the advantages
of his place in history.   They enable an individual
to take possession of the inheritance that has been
accumulated for him.*

If what I have said is true, it ought to follow
that in proportion as a man is untutored he is
not a man of his age at all.   He might just as
well have been born a thousand years ago.   Suppose a child to be kept altogether from educative
influences, simply fed and kept alive, and he
would not belong to the present any more than
to the past.   He would have no place in history at all.   It would be as absurd to speak of
him as modern as it would be to speak of the
modern whale or the modern ant.   While no individual has ever been cut off altogether from the
spirit of his age, I think any one will readily agree
that this is in a large measure true of millions
of our fellow men.   And one will agree, I think,
that, in principle, being a man of the age depends
upon the enjoyment of educational opportunities.
Illiteracy, grinding toil, rigid customs, physical
remoteness, lack of facilities for communication,
imply stagnation in a primitive, monotonous and

timeless animal existence. There are millions of peasants and laborers who enter upon a mechanical routine of life, driven by the necessity of livelihood, without ever having had a chance to acquire and utilize the accumulations of the past. They live and die as genuinely cut off and disinherited from the history of civilization as their cattle or beasts of burden.

There is another class who acquire the *fashions* of their age, but nothing more. Such men get just so much of the life of their times as can be derived from superficial contact and external imitation. They become men of the modern age in so far as this consists in using current slang, singing topical songs, wearing clothes of a conventional pattern and being familiar with the latest material conveniences. Externally, they are up to date; internally, they are simply human animals belonging to no time, and none the richer by the accident of being born here and now.

Viewed in the light of these facts, a liberal education should be regarded as the means of introducing the younger generation to its birthright, a sort of visiting the ancestral estate before taking possession. The best example of what I mean is afforded by historical studies,

not only history in the usual sense of political
history, but history as a record of man's past
achievements in art, science, industry, and religion.   The study of history in this sense is like
pausing on one's journey to take a long look
backward, so that one may see the direction of
one's way, and realize vividly the place one has
reached.   And through history, one takes over
the past and makes it one's own.   One becomes
so connected with the past, that one can be said
to carry it on, or to begin where it leaves off.
It is like running a relay race; when one's turn
comes, one has to touch the last runner in order
to take up the race in his stead, inheriting at the
start the advantage that he and others before
him have earned.   Historical studies are a sort
of touching of the past by which one claims one's
place in the race, and runs not in the first but in
the third or fourth millennium.

   The first characteristic of liberal studies, then,
is their affording a retrospect of civilization,
giving the individual an opportunity to claim
the past of mankind as his own past, and starting him abreast of his times.   The extent to which
one values a liberal education will so far depend
upon the extent to which one wishes to claim
one's title to the accumulated learning, experience

and achievements of man, or is satisfied to be disinherited—a person of no time, enjoying no point of vantage in the scale of progress.

Let us turn to a second characteristic. I have been using the phrase "liberal studies" without explaining the meaning of the word "liberal." It means "free" or "generous." But why does one speak of studies as free, or generous? In contrast, I take it, with studies in which one is constrained by routine, or by the need of livelihood. But there is a more positive sense in which certain studies may be said to be free: in the sense, namely, of *making free*, or of increasing freedom.

It seems fairly obvious that freedom is somehow proportional to the range of alternatives from which we may choose. If, as we say, "we have no other alternative," then what we do is the *only thing* we can do and is, therefore, necessary. Similarly, we say of a man, "He never had a chance to do otherwise," and find in that fact evidence of lack of freedom. Now, there is nothing that limits and reduces freedom so commonly as ignorance. In order that things shall be real alternatives for our choice, we have got to know about them; the things we have never heard of

are the things we have never had the least chance
of doing. It follows that a wide range of knowledge—knowing about a great many things—
multiplies our freedom and increases the extent
to which we may be said to do what we really
want rather than what circumstance dictates.
What civilization makes possible, education may
make real; for liberal education here again is
what really brings the individual and the civilization of his age together. Viewed in this light,
liberal education is a wide survey of the field of
life, a broad outlook over all its manifold possibilities, so that one may *choose* in the presence
of all the varied possibilities.

The most far-reaching choice that a man
makes is the choice of work. To a very large
extent, far more so than we ordinarily understand, the work dictates to the man, *when once
he undertakes it*. A job is a hard master. There
is just one moment at which the job is not the
master, and that is the moment at which one
chooses the job. Hence, if one never deliberately
chooses the job, but simply grows up to it, or falls
into it by accident, or is thrust into it by others
or by the pressure of need, then one loses forever
that moment of freedom. There is a sense in
which everybody has a job sooner or later. It

need not be one of the regularly defined profes-
sions or trades. But one finds a place somewhere
in the world's work, and once in the place, the
work is, as we say, "cut out" for one. If one is
to be free, then, one must be conscious, alive to
the situation, and in some measure, at least,
choose for oneself the work that one shall do.
And the more completely one is aware of the
varied possibilities which life affords, the freer
is one's choice.

Liberal education, then, is the sort of education that helps one to choose one's work freely,
rather than the kind of education that fits one
for one's chosen work. The traditional view that
one's college days are the days in which one
should be *deciding what to do* is essentially correct. And the studies which one pursues should
be primarily those which present the alternatives
in all their multiplicity and variety. They should
enable one for the moment to take a *general
view* before one descends into the plain and takes
one's place. For in the plain, such general views
are rare, and it is harder to profit by them
even when one has them. "It is not the intention of Nature," says Emerson, "that one should
live by general views. We fetch fire and water,
run about all day among the shops, and markets,

and get our clothes and shoes made and mended, and are the victims of these details, and once in a fortnight we arrive, perhaps, at a rational moment." The period of liberal education should be the greatest of such rational moments, the lucid interval, when we look all about, spy out the promised land, and are for once free.

It follows that this period of liberal study may well be a period of desultory attention, of a sort of spiritual idling and irresponsibility, when according to the standards of efficiency, time is wasted. To look back upon one's college days from the standpoint of an established position in the world, and say: "My college studies have not helped me to succeed," is to betray an utterly wrong notion as to the essential purpose of college education. It was their essential purpose not to prepare one to succeed in the practise of law, for example, but to help one to decide wisely and freely *whether to aspire to such success*. Consulting the time-table does not help you to catch your train, but it does play an important part in your deciding what train to catch. Among other things, it shows you what trains there are to catch, and the destinations to which they are likely to carry you.

It is clear that one cannot judge the value of

a liberal education by the standards of success
or efficiency. It is quite essential to its value
that one should hold such standards in abeyance.
It requires an attitude quite different from that
which is required by the actual contest of life,
as different as the attitude of the general who
plans a campaign is different from his attitude
when he executes it. Once the forward movement is on, what is required is courage, persis-
tence, skill, patience, and single-minded devotion to the matter in hand. These are the virtues of *action*. But other virtues are required
in the time of deliberation and counsel, such
virtues as imagination, breadth of view, and
statesmanship. To profit most by liberal study
or to acquire that which is peculiarly valuable in
it, one needs freedom and elasticity of mind, the
proverbial "generosity of youth," openness of
mind, quickness of response, a toleration of the
most ancient heresies, and an eager interest in
the most radical novelties; so that for once,
albeit for only a fleeting moment, all things shall
have presented themselves and had their chance
of acceptance or rejection.

There are few branches of knowledge that
may not be liberal studies if only they be taken
in this spirit. What I have said does not argue

for a narrowing of the curriculum to the study of the ancient languages. On the contrary, as William James has said, "we must shake the old double reefs out of the canvas into the wind and sunshine, and let in every modern subject, sure that any subject will prove humanistic, if its setting be kept only wide enough." For a liberal education means, primarily, a retrospect of the past, an assimilation of the civilization of one's age, and a wide acquaintance with the possibilities of life, in order that choice of vocation may be wise and free.

XI

THE USELESS VIRTUES

IF all the good advice that has ever been given were to be brought together and compared, it would probably be discovered that every piece could be matched with a contrary piece given by somebody else. The world's practical wisdom does not form a consistent system. No one man could possibly believe all of it at the same time. For example, there is equally good authority for believing that woman is the tyrant of man, and for believing that she is his puppet. Victor Hugo tells us that "men are women's playthings; woman is the devil's"; while another Frenchman, Michelet, tells us that "nearly every folly committed by woman is born of the stupidity or evil influence of man." But it may be argued that in this case it is the very paradox itself which is proverbial. Take the less familiar example of self-consciousness. There are the moralists whose primary maxim is the Delphic oracle, "Know thyself." "We should every night call ourselves to an account," says Seneca. "What infirmity have I mastered to-day? What passion opposed? What temptation resisted? What virtue acquired? Our vices will abate of themselves if they be brought every day to the shrift." This is accounted wise, and carries conviction to conscience. But so does the contrary preaching of Carlyle, with his tirade against the "unhealthy state of self-sentience, self-survey, precursor and prognostic of still worse health."

It is painful to contemplate the volume of discordant advice that is poured from pulpits, platforms and editorial columns into the ears of that hapless reprobate, the plain man. It is perhaps fortunate that so little of it is followed, for it is always one-sided. It is characteristic of most advice and exhortation that it is only a part of the truth. It is an exaggeration of that particular half-truth which the exhorter thinks is timely, and which he believes is going to be offset by contrary influences. It is a push against some existing overtendency, an attempt to stem some tide that is running too high, in the hope of securing that balance and moderation in which right conduct always consists.

This is my apology for appearing with an exhortation which on the face of it may appear to be strained or even absurd. For I propose, in a sense, to preach *against efficiency or success*. I do so not because I do not see their importance, but because I suspect that my reader will already know their importance well enough, and possibly even too well. Or if he does not, there are many who can proclaim that importance more eloquently than I. There is something abroad, an irresistible social impulse, which is tending to promote the useful virtues, to encourage thrift, initiative, industry, co-operation, civic pride, and all those qualities of mind and will that make communities sound and prosperous. But were I to join the general praise of efficiency and utility, I should be seeing only half the truth. And I know that, if I were to follow the line of less resistance and urge what everybody already wants, I should be forfeiting the greater opportunity of speaking a word for that half-truth which has difficulty in getting a hearing and needs the strong support of every teacher or preacher. I want, therefore, to make out as strong a case as I can for what may in a sense be called *the useless virtues*, for those qualities of mind and will which cannot be measured by the standard of efficiency —whose very value, indeed, is inseparable from the fact that they do not immediately contribute to practical success.

First of all it is necessary that we should reflect upon the meaning of a word that is perpetually in our mouths—the word "practical." It is not customary for us to reflect upon its meaning at all. It is supposed to express a finality. To call a thing practical is to praise it; to call it unpractical is to condemn it. It never occurs to us as a rule that practicality is a special kind of value. If that did occur to us, then, of course, we should be in the position of admitting that there is at least one other kind of value from which it may be distinguished. And this would be equivalent to admitting that when we call a thing practical or unpractical we have not, as is usually assumed, provided sufficient grounds for approving or rejecting it.

Let me select a homely example which will bring out what appears to me to be the meaning of practicality. Suppose a man to be driven to the roof of a burning building, while a crowd is gathered below to offer help or suggestions. Jones shouts, "Get a ladder!" or indicates where one may be had, or gets one himself. Brown points out an adjacent roof by which the refugee may pass to a place of safety. Several Smiths fetch a blanket and hold it to break his fall. Socrates who has happened by, and who appears to be less agitated than the rest, remarks (largely to himself, for he can find few to listen to him): "I wonder what the man really wants. He appears to be desperately anxious to save his life. But is his life after all so prodigiously important as to warrant all this excitement? Has he good reasons for wishing to save himself? And what a poorly organized community is this, where such a thing should be allowed to occur! Why are buildings not fireproof? What carelessness can have started the fire?" But before Socrates can proceed further with his ruminations he is roughly brushed aside. If he receives any consideration at all he will be regarded as a poor lunatic, or philosopher, or college professor.

Now, which among these men is the practical man, and which the unpractical? I do not suppose that there can be the slightest doubt in any one's mind. The Joneses, the Browns, and the Smiths are the practical men, and Socrates (there is rarely even one such in any crowd) is theoretical, academic, a creature of mere intellect; harmless enough if he will only stay at home and write books which nobody reads, but very much in the way when there is something to be done.

But what is the precise difference between the

Joneses, the Browns, and the Smiths on the one hand, and Socrates on the other? It appears to me that it comes down to this. The practical men accept circumstances as they find them. They take it for granted that the man wants to escape from the roof; and they regard the fire as an existing fact which is not, for the moment at least, to be explained, but to be acted on. They do not go behind this concrete and present situation, except so far as to assume on the victim's part the normal instinct of self-preservation. Taking these things for granted, without consciously reflecting upon them at all, they can devote all their faculties and energies to contriving a remedy. In so far as their minds are engaged at all they will be bent upon finding the means that will fit the situation. In this way the problem is enormously simplified, and there is strong likelihood of a prompt and effectual solution. If the crowd were made up entirely of Socrateses pondering all the whys and wherefores, life would be lost before any conclusions whatsoever would have been reached. To be practical, in short, is to confine one's attention to the effectual meeting of existing emergencies.

President Cleveland invented a phrase which is an almost perfect expression of the attitude of practicality.   There is nothing profound about it, nor does it possess any striking literary merit; but it never fails to appeal, and has become a part of our common speech, so thoroughly does it coincide with the bias of common sense. He once remarked, as every one knows: "It is a condition, and not a theory, that confronts us." I do not remember what condition it was that confronted us; but the practical man is always confronted by a condition. I shall suggest presently that every condition does in truth involve a theory; but if so, the practical man ignores it. His practicality lies in confining himself to finding an act which will meet the condition. He has a family which must be supported, or an industrial plant which must be made to pay, or an examination which must be passed, or a game which must be won, or an office to which he proposes to be elected. His problem is the comparatively narrow and simple problem of finding the instrument to fit the occasion and achieve the result.

As a nation, we are commonly accused by unsympathetic Europeans of being excessively practical. We are supposed to specialize in practicality. Thus, when England wants a railroad system reorganized she looks to America for a manager, and when Germany wants to make a better record in the Olympic games she sends to America for a trainer. There is less demand in Europe for American poets and musical composers, and, I regret to say, for American philosophers. Now we may believe that this reputation is not deserved, or we may glory in it. But in either case we can afford at least to see just what it means. Consider for a moment the verdict of one of our harshest critics, Mr. G. Lowes Dickinson, of Cambridge University. "I am inclined to think," he says, "that the real end which Americans set before themselves is Acceleration. To be always moving, and always moving faster, that they think is the beatific life; and with their happy detachment from philosophy and speculation, they are not troubled by the question, Whither? If they are asked by Europeans, as they sometimes are, what is the point of going so fast? their only feeling is one of genuine astonishment. Why, they reply, you go fast! And what more can be said?"[1]

Now no doubt this is a libel upon the American people, and might justly be resented. Or it might perhaps be proved that Mr. Dickinson's fellow countrymen are just as guilty in intent as

[1] *A Modern Symposium*, pp. 104-105.

we are. Perhaps they want to move fast, but, failing to do it, try to make out that the game isn't worth the candle, and that their rival's victory is hollow and fruitless; as a man who saw that he was losing a race might withdraw and try to persuade the spectators that it was a very childish and undignified proceeding anyhow. There would doubtless be a dash of truth in such a retort, just enough to enable you to get the laugh on the other fellow. But it would be a shrewder thing to detect the truth in the criticism, learn one's fault, correct it, and leave the critic himself to stagnate in his own complacency.

Now Mr. Dickinson's criticism brings out cleverly enough the meaning of that practicality on which we pride ourselves, and which we hastily assume to be an absolute standard. Practicality means skill, energy, speed, quantity of performance, without reference to the profitableness of the result. Not that the result may not in point of fact be profitable; the question simply is not raised. The profitableness of the result is assumed from the fact that everybody is mad about it. As the popular song puts it, "everybody's doing it." Whatever everybody is doing recommends itself without further justification. Whatever everybody's doing is "the thing to do."

A man is willing to wear anything apparently, if his tailor says, "they're wearing them that way." So we eagerly adopt the pursuits that we find in vogue, and apply ourselves to making a good showing.

Most people, perhaps, appear to be dividing their energies between three pursuits: making money, dancing, and playing baseball or watching some one else play it. To make as much money as possible, to dance as well or as often as possible, and to defeat your opponent in sport, either personally or vicariously through a favorite team—these tasks absorb the energies of the typical practical man. He does not adopt and follow a plan of life by conscious reflection, but he is constantly in a current of life, which flows now this way and now that, and sweeps him along with it. Or the practical man is like a man who finds himself in a great throng of athletes who are matching their skill and speed and prowess against one another. He goes in for this or that, spurred by emulation, and seeks to outstrip his competitors in some race without concerning himself with the direction of the course and the place in which he will find himself at the end of the race.

There is a false proverb which teaches us that whatever is worth doing is worth doing well.

I call it false because it is so evident that there are some things which are only worth doing provided one is willing to do them ill. It is a part of practical wisdom to know what it is worth while to exert oneself about, and what may be done in a spirit of playful carelessness. But there is a more popular maxim which is so widely observed that it is never formulated—the maxim that whatever is done well is worth doing. This, I take it, is the maxim of the practical man. Do what the next man is doing, but go him one better. Make a record. There is a whole code of life in this passion for records. To make or hold a record means to excel everybody else in a precisely measurable degree. To excel everybody else in an activity in which everybody else would like to excel, *to hold the most coveted record*, this would represent the supreme practical success.

We should now be sufficiently clear in our minds as to what practicality means. But it is evident that our critics in judging us to be a peculiarly practical people mean to accuse us of a fault, and we shall not have understood the criticism until we have come to see wherein the fault lies. It is evident that Mr. Dickinson, for example, means to convey the idea that this question, Whither?—which is said to trouble us so little—is an important question, and that we are making a serious mistake in ignoring it. He would mean, I think, to go further, and assert that this question, Whither? is the *most* important question.

When we examine the matter more narrowly, it appears to come to this. The very same instance of successful effort may be glorious or ridiculous, according as the result is itself worth while or not. I remember an adventure of my own that is in point. I left Cambridge with a friend to catch a six-o'clock boat for Portland, Maine. We had been delayed in starting and upon consulting our watches in the car we found that unless we adopted extraordinary measures we should miss the boat. So we leaped from the car and hailed a passing cab. We bribed the driver to whip his horse into a gallop. As we approached the dock we saw the boat moving. Jumping from the cab with bags in hand, we ran down the dock and leaped aboard, flushed with our triumph. We had exerted ourselves desperately; we had been quick-witted and skilful, and I suspect that we had created a record. We had certainly succeeded. But when our excitement and breathlessness subsided we discovered that the boat *was just arriving*, and that it would not depart for several hours. Then something very extraordinary happened to our triumph. It suddenly collapsed and shrivelled into a sorry joke. We felt ashamed and ridiculous, and sought to hide our diminished heads in the impersonal throng of bystanders.

I wonder if there is any better definition of that most hateful of predicaments, which we describe as "having made a fool of oneself," than to say that it is *to have exerted oneself for an end that turns out to be worthless in the attainment*. Suppose a man to have devoted himself passionately to the accumulation of riches, to have spent himself, literally, in getting them, and to have prided himself on his skill and efficiency, only to find that the riches do not amount to anything when he has them; so that although he has been so extraordinarily busy in doing, he has in reality done nothing. Such a man might well feel in the flat and empty years of his ebbing life that he had played the fool, and that he might better have been less busy, if only he might then have taken a little time to think ahead and select some worthy goal before throwing himself headlong into the pursuit.

A moment's thought about the ends themselves, looking before you leap, curiously inquiring into the itinerary before joining the procession, a little cool philosophy before the heat of action, *disinterested reflection*, these are what I mean by the useless virtues—the unpractical wisdom of Socrates. Surely such wisdom has its place. You cannot make life up out of it altogether. Socrates in his most Socratic moods will not make an effective member of the fire brigade. There are times for action, and when they come the man of the hour is he who has no doubts, but only instincts and habits. Our instincts and habits, however, take care of themselves better than does our cool reflection. The mood of practicality is the vulgar mood; not in the sense of being debased, but in the sense of being usual or typical. For the individual it is the line of less resistance. Being usual, it sets the standards by which a man is judged by the crowd. It is favored by that popular prejudice called common sense. It requires no exhortation of mine in order to get a hearing. Therefore I urge, doubtless with some exaggeration, the value of the rarer but not less indispensable mood.

It would seem that practical efficiency and disinterested reflection might then divide life between them, each having its appropriate season, and each requiring in society at large its special organs and devotees. But since we are for the moment the partisans of disinterested reflection, let us recognize a certain advantage that it has over its rival—the advantage, namely, of magnanimity. I mean that while disinterested reflection acknowledges the merit of its rival, practical efficiency in its haste and narrow bent is likely to be blind and intolerant. If I were asked, "What, in the name of common sense, is philosophy?" I should be unable to answer. There is no answer. For amongst the categories of common sense there is no provision for philosophy. With a person wholly dominated by common sense, caught and swept along in the tide of practical endeavor, or wholly dominated by social habit, the philosophical part is in disuse and may be atrophied altogether. But if I ask, "What, in the name of philosophy, is common sense?" I can find an answer—just such an answer perhaps as we are now giving. In short, disinterested reflection is more inclusive, and more circumspect, than practicality.

But I have not even yet exhausted the peculiar merits of the unpractical value of disinterested reflection. I have spoken of its importance as testing the value of ends, and so confirming or discrediting our more impetuous practical endeavor. But there is another point. I refer to the advantage of unapplied knowledge as giving man resourcefulness and adaptability, a capacity to meet novel situations. Let me attempt to make my meaning clear.

We praise science in these days, and most of us prefer it to poetry or philosophy, because we can see the *use of it*. It is characteristic of our practical standards that we regard such men as Watts, Bell, Morse and Edison as typifying the value of science. The inventor, the engineer, is the man of solid achievement. Why? Because, again, he supplies that for which the need is already felt. We want light, communication and transportation, and such men as these give us what we want. Therefore we are grateful. Similarly, the man who discovers a cure for cancer will be a hero among men. There is a powerful demand, an eager longing for that which he will have to give, and his reward will be ready for him when he comes.

Now we need not disparage his glory. But this is perfectly certain: when the discovery is made, it will be due to the store of physical, chemical, physiological, and anatomical truth which has been accumulated by men who were animated mainly by theoretical motives. These investigators have devoted themselves to winning knowledge for which there was at the time no practical demand. This means that they had to be sustained by something else than the popular applause which greets the man with the remedy. Such men are sustained no doubt by the encouragement of their fellow investigators, or by the patronage of the state. But they rely more than the inventor or engineer upon the inward support of their own love of truth, and upon a certain just pride of the intellect, such as Kepler felt when he wrote in the Preface to his *Weltharmonik*: "Here I cast the die, and write a book to be read, whether by contemporaries or by posterity, I care not; it can wait for readers thousands of years, seeing that God himself waited six thousand years for some one to contemplate his work."

But I had not meant to be sentimental about it, or to claim a greater heroism for the detached investigator. Indeed there is a sense in which his conduct is less praiseworthy, in so far as it is often self-regarding or unsocial, lacking in that motive of service which we rightly require of perfect conduct. It is sufficient that we should see that what he does is indispensable. It is

through his efforts that man is put into possession of a stock of free and unappropriated ideas
with which to meet unexpected and unpredictable
emergencies, or on which to construct new hypoth-
eses. It is this possession of an ample margin
of knowledge over the recognized practical neces-
sities, of *intellectual capital*, so to speak, that is
the condition of progress. It is this which more
than anything else marks the difference between
man and the brute, or between progressive societies and those static, barbarian societies in
which human energy is exhausted by the effort
to preserve existence with no hope of betterment.

It is now evident enough that what I have
called useless virtues, or unpractical values, are
not divorced from life in any absolute or ultimate
sense. We may as well declare once and for all
that there is no virtue or value whatsoever that
is divorced from life in such a sense. That it is
impossible that knowledge should be absolutely
useless is self-evident. For to know at all is to
know the world we live in, and to know it is to
bring it within the range of action, pave the way
to the control of it. The better we know our
world the more effectually we can live in it. This
holds unqualifiedly. But there is a very great

difference between what we might more correctly call *long-range* and *short-range* practicality.

What we usually speak of as practical would correspond to what I here speak of as short-range practicality. It means a readiness to meet the immediate occasion as is dictated by the momentary desire. Such practicality is a perpetual meeting of emergencies. It is a sort of living from hand to mouth, an uninspired and unillumined opportunism. That which is ordinarily condemned as unpractical, and which *is* unpractical from this *narrow* standpoint, may now be called long-range practicality. That is to say, it is that prevision, that thorough intellectual equipment, that wisdom as to the ultimate and comparative worth of things, without which there can be no security nor any confirming sense of genuine achievement. It is that which makes the difference between making a fool of oneself, however earnestly or even successfully, and living in a manner which would be able to endure the test of time.

XII

THE CONDESCENDING MAN AND THE OBSTRUCTIVE WOMAN

CAN the free man, in keeping with his code of freedom, deny that prerogative to women? It is a very personal matter, and as public issues go, a relatively simple matter. Let us put it as concretely as possible. Your neighbor has asked that her voice be heard and that her will be counted in deciding some matter of general neighborhood policy, such, for example, as the construction of a new street. It so happens that this particular neighbor has a very lively interest in the matter, being, let us say, the owner of property through which the projected street would pass. She asks you to consent to some change of procedure that will enable her to represent her own interest and to have her will count as one among the rest. Your first impulse is to smile—the outward expression of your feeling of incongruity. Such a smile is the restrained way of manifesting that delicate derision with which irregularity is greeted by the perfectly habituated. It is what remains when civilization has refined away the boorish laughter with which the natural man condemns a breach of custom or departure from the familiar type. You have been used to settling affairs with men whose wives you have met only in those lighter pastimes known as "society."

But after the first shock the realities of the situation press upon you. Your neighbor's request is irresistibly natural and reasonable. Unless you are a trained casuist you will not hesitate to admit her "right" to be heard and counted. It will come over you that her sex, while it affects the amenities and proprieties, has nothing to do with the merits of her claim. Has she a vital interest in the outcome? Has she a matured opinion? Is she capable of discussion? Then what under heaven has her *sex* to do with it? Thus qualified she has made good her title to rule among the rest, even though she is a daughter of Eve. You will have no difficulty in recalling the names of several sons of Adam whose qualifications are more doubtful, but whose title is not challenged because it has been thought less dangerous to enfranchise one hundred whose title is doubtful than to disfranchise one whose title is clear. Better excessive liberality than the suspicion of tyranny.

Out of such reflections as these, if you are honest-minded and more concerned with the substance than with the form of the thing, there will grow a recognition of your neighbor as fellow-citizen. You will come to see that *rights* and *interests* and *reasoned conviction* are neither masculine nor feminine. You may even accustom your eyes to petticoats at the council-table, and your ear to the close succession of the words "votes" and "women." The impulse to smile may be forgotten in an unself-conscious effort to work out the common good. You will have found an association of minds and purposes where at first you saw only a bit of comedy. And when you meet your neighbor in that conference in which she registers her will among the rest, you may even have so far regained your composure as to be able to remove your hat.

This, then, is the question. It is a neighborhood question between one human being and another. There are no immutable political axioms from which it can be argued. All of its realities, and all of the evidence that is germane and decisive are to be found in the concrete situation in which human interests and human minds are associated. To grasp the larger and vaguer issue, you must reduce it in scale and express it in terms of your own immediate community. "Rights" come into existence when human beings assert them and other human beings acknowledge them. The rights of women are now in the making; they are being generated by the natural and irresistible growth of practises and ideas to which we have long been committed. You cannot deny your neighbor; no man can deny his neighbor. In your act of acknowledgment your neighbor acquires a right; by such an acknowledgment repeated a million times, a whole social class is enfranchised.

This is a question between men and women, not between Man and Woman. Each individual must translate it for himself into terms of his own personal relations. Recall to mind the wisest and best woman of your acquaintance. Forget convention and legalized usage, and remember only that she has interests as genuine as yours, purposes as broad and benevolent, and opinions that to her seem true even as do yours to you. She wishes to participate in the regulation of public policies in a community that is assumed to be self-governing. She possesses interests that belong to the community of interests which government is designed to promote; she has opinions and is able to express them, in a polity that is founded on the principle of government by discussion and agreement. It happens that you enjoy *de facto* political power and that it is only through your consent that she can represent her interests and make her opinion effective.

When you present the case to yourself thus concretely and personally, are there no sentiments of justice and respect that instantly prescribe what shall be your course? Can you in the presence of such an individual, conscious of her interests, articulate in her judgment, soberly demanding what she conceives to be her just rights, still wear upon your face that smile with which you dispose of the matter in her absence?

I, for one, cannot. I have no heart for banter and pleasantry in the face of conscious and intentional seriousness. I could not carry it through. I should be overtaken with shame at my own insolence. Or can you allow your face to wear the aspect of offended taste? As for me, I cannot. The bathos of it is too intolerable. Can you in such a presence enter with conviction upon a discussion of the relation of abstract Right to abstract Woman? I could not go far without feeling that I was getting pedantic and irrelevant. I know so much better what I owe to this woman, than I or anybody else knows the ultimate philosophy of the ballot. Can you deny her from mere love of power? If so, you will not admit it. Tyranny must nowadays wear a mask. The honest tyrant who says, "I have this power and I do not choose to divide and reduce it," is obsolete. If he were not we should know how to deal with him. But he is masked, and unless we look sharp we shall not recognize him. He is most beguiling as The Condescending Man. It is worth while to know him well in that rôle, for thus disguised he is all about us.

The Condescending Man is the self-conscious and self-constituted guardian of woman. If his carriage is a little pompous, if he is a little lacking in the qualities of comradeship, we must forgive him that since it comes of the very abundance of his virtue. He beams with good-will and with gracious tolerance of the foibles of his ward. She may even bite and scratch, and he will spoil her. She may even protest that she does not want his guardianship, and he will forgive her; for how can she be expected to know what is good for her! He must be patient even when misunderstood, and must serve even the ungrateful against their will.   If they but knew, how they would thank him!   In the editorial columns of the New York *Times* he is positively magnanimous.[1] "No upright and decent man desires to withhold from woman any privilege which will benefit her"—"*any* privilege," mark you!   Could any devotion be more perfect?   He will go out "into the everlasting scrimmage of life" in order that she may foster her "charm and tenderness" at home, or radiate it in the cloistered schoolroom.

To argue the disfranchisement of women one must deny to the sex as a whole some quality with which men are by nature endowed.   To accomplish this without arrogance it is necessary to make as little as possible of man's prerogative; which results in disparaging not only the prerogative, but also the province for which it qualifies him.   That which men alone are fitted to do, which women are constitutionally incapable of doing, must to a chivalrous mind seem a relatively ignoble thing to do.   Hence the distinctive mark of man is his animal virility, and the province for which he is fitted is the "*fera mœnia militiai* and the no less rude task of politics."[2]

---

[1] February 7, 1915.
[2] Professor E. K. Rand, in *Harper's Weekly*, October 30, 1915.

But this is to assume that shallow opinion of politics by which some of the more fastidious of the Virile Animals excuse their own political indolence. It does not come of reflecting deeply on the function of the state or the ethics of citizenship. Plato, having distinguished between the "rudeness" which is "the natural product of the spirited element" and the "gentleness" which is "a property of the philosophical temperament," proposes that "the class of philosophers be invested with the supreme authority in a state." For Plato, in short, the supreme political qualification is not hardiness and daring, but philosophy —which, whatever its shortcomings, is certainly not a display of rude animal virility!

Is it not time for us to banish altogether this American provincialism, which conceives politics as a square-jawed, bull-necked occupation requiring calloused hands and a strong stomach? Can there be any act to which mere animal virility is less appropriate than the act of social self-government? Is there any act which calls higher spiritual qualities into play? Citizenship is a matter not for brawn but for brains, not for physical, but for moral, courage. It puts a strain not on body but on character. It is because I know women to possess these essential qualifications for citizenship, and because I know that they possess some of them pre-eminently, such as humanity and the power to endure, that I cannot but concede to women the full rights of citizenship.

Politics is discussion and organization for the general good. Shall men deny to women participation in these matters because men have so conducted them as to make their purpose obscure and their name odious? The tone of political affairs is given to them by the quality of those who conduct them. The Condescending Man's poor opinion of their tone would suggest that they may have been left too largely in the hands of Virile Animals. Even he would not propose that the charm and tenderness which occasionally manifest themselves even among men should be regarded as excusing them from political life. In short, if one is to argue at all from the rudeness of political life, the conclusion would be, not that the higher humanity should be kept from politics, but rather that politics should be more highly humanized.

In these days of rough force The Condescending Man stands almost alone in his charity and considerate regard. He is benevolent through and through, and he doesn't care who knows it. God bless him! No one with a heart in his bosom can remain untouched at such a spectacle. It is little wonder that many of his grateful wards rise up and call him blessed, asking no happier lot than to enjoy· his protection, his caressing kindness, and the light of his infallible wisdom.

It is ungracious to probe into the motives of a benevolence so perfect. Such a task is not willingly undertaken even by his less inspired fellow guardians, who owe him no debt of gratitude. But let us shake off the spell, and remember as vividly as we can just how it feels to be amiably but persistently treated as a ward, when one doesn't want to be a ward. Every man has experienced the difficulty of getting his majority acknowledged by those who have long regarded him as a child. There comes a time in every man's life when what he wants is not indulgence or even provident care, but independence. This painful struggle, the inevitable and recurrent tragedy of father and son, is not a struggle over benefits withheld or bestowed, but over the right to judge what *are* benefits. An adult is a person who is the acknowledged authority as to what he himself wants. He is willing to forfeit good-will or even good deeds, for the sake of being allowed to say for himself what is good. Such relations and such struggles occur in every association of older and younger men. There comes a time sooner or later when benevolent paternalism is unduly prolonged, and becomes an intolerable restraint upon liberty. When such is the case the benevolent patron is in danger of having his feelings hurt. His misguided and belated providence can no longer be gratefully accepted, but must be firmly and regretfully overthrown.

Something of this sort, I take it, is involved in the present painful misunderstanding between some men and some women. There are women who believe that they are grown up, and who are trying to get the fact acknowledged. They are not seeking what is good for them, but they would like to be regarded as competent to decide what *is* good for them. Their most formidable obstacle is the man who is quite firmly convinced that *he* knows what is good for them. His intentions are good, and his habits of mind, inherited from the usage of the past, are quite inflexible. There arises the painful necessity of disregarding his good intentions, or even of resenting them in order to gain the main point. He on his part will find his habits of mind unsuited to the new relationship, and will cling to them in order to avoid awkwardness and loss of dignity. He will inevitably feel abused that his good intentions should not have been deemed sufficient.

At the risk of further injury to his feelings let us examine a little more closely into the motives of The Condescending Man. I do not want to be cynical—but why does he so *insist* upon his benevolence, even when it is so ungratefully received? Is it possible that there is some satisfaction in the provident care of dependents, and that he becomes aware of it, and clings to it at the moment when he is about to lose it? I strongly suspect that such is the case. Indeed upon careful introspection I am sure of it. A benign graciousness reciprocated by an attitude of grateful and trusting dependence and pervaded by a thoroughly good conscience, distils one of the most delicious of pleasures—a pleasure not to be abandoned without a struggle. It exists in forms far subtler than the rough triumph of a Petruchio; but it requires that Katharine shall be tamed and shall remain so. This same exquisite sentiment inspires those who regret the passing of the "good servant." This departed blessing is a creature grateful for the advantages of "a refined home" (even though it happens to be somebody else's home) and content to receive benefits selected and doled out by her acknowledged superiors. In the golden age of patronage men could patronize domesticated women while these in turn could exercise their benevolence upon domesticated servants. And now the outlook for all patrons is bad, owing to the wide-spread and growing dislike of being patronized.

The Condescending Man is fond of his condescension. He cannot bear to give it up. He resists a change that will rob it of his object. The good old practise of deciding what is good for other people, of prescribing it and spooning it out with kindly smiles is in grave danger. It cannot possibly be carried on unless there is a being at hand who will open her mouth, swallow her sugared dose, and look pleased while she does it. It is a highly gratifying thing to exchange descending benevolence with ascending gratitude. The downward slant of condescension must encounter the upward inclination of dependence. Otherwise it has no fulcrum and can only waste itself in space. The horizontal interchange of friendship isn't the same thing at all. Hence The Condescending Man quite naturally, too naturally, goes about praising and promoting the ob-

ject which he needs for the exercise of his condescension.

I have tried to do justice to The Condescending Man, and to give him due credit for his good
intentions. But I feel compelled to admit that
he sometimes appears in a less amiable light. He
has even been known to hint strongly that his
indulgent care for women is a sort of compensa-
tion to them for their lack of political power.
If they prefer to possess political power, then
they must make up their minds to give up their
immunity from military service and jury duty,
their dower rights, their legal claims to support
and to alimony, and the protection of their
health by special factory laws. "Equal rights,
equal duties," says our editorial friend,[1] by
way of showing that even The Condescending
Man can be firm if it should prove necessary.

It might have been supposed that these "privileges" of women were based upon differences of
physical strength and aptitude; and upon the peculiar services which women render to society by
the bearing and rearing of children, and by the
immediate care of the home. These have some-

[1] New York *Times*, February 28, 1915.

times been regarded as duties quite "equal" to fighting and bread-winning. In that case the formula would have to be amended to read "equal rights, *identical* duties," which is somewhat less axiomatic. In any case the principle of benevolence is here abandoned for that of bargaining. And the bargain is proposed by the party that has the upper hand and believes itself to be in a position to dictate terms. Condescension is here prescribing conditions, as though one were to say: "I will give you what I think is good for you, but only provided you will accept certain existing disabilities—I will give freely, but you must pay for it."

Similarly, a defender of the privileges of men has proposed the inverted sentiment: "No representation without taxation." Since women as a class are too frail to bear the burdens of politics and war, they "should not have the right to vote about them." But one who employs this argument either has an inadequate conception of politics and war or he has an inadequate conception of the public service of women. Since his chivalry acquits him of the latter, we must convict him of the former. He is betrayed, I think, by a conventional and antiquated conception of politics and war. That he regards politics under its superficial and local aspect, and confuses its abuses with its uses, we have already found reason to suspect. If he were to remind himself that politics is concerted action for the public interest, he would find it less incongruous with his conception of womanliness.

Similarly he appears to identify war with the shock of arms, despite the fact that recent events have relegated this idea to the class of picture-book anachronisms. War is the organization and mobilization of a nation's resources. War is the care of fatherless children; war is food and clothing, science and invention, nursing and sanitation, diplomacy and literature. When war is thus conceived the participation of women is not questionable at all. They do participate. Their loyalty is stanch, their industry unremitting, and their burden more heavy than the most generous man has ever fully acknowledged. There is only one symbol of civil rights, one instrument of political autonomy—the vote. There are a thousand forms of service, equally burdensome. The day has passed when it can be lightly said that women are to be denied the former on the ground that they do not assume a proportionate share of the latter.

I fear that The Condescending Man's code of

manners, like his code of morals, is also tainted
with the spirit of barter. There are rumors that
if women enjoy too many privileges he may feel
compelled to sit in their presence with his hat
on, by way of showing that the bargain is off.
That is to say, courtesy rests on a tacit contract
by which the recipient is bound to give up more
substantial advantages in return. "Ladies First"
means that women are to be given precedence in
non-essentials on the understanding that they
yield it in essentials. They may sit in the draw-
ing-room or even the tram-car, provided they
will confine themselves to the gallery in the hall
of legislation. Such is the code of The Condescending Man. Now it is interesting to note,
as a curious social phenomenon, that some men
in some parts of the world even practise courtesy
to one another! This sometimes goes even to
the point of the removal of hats and the yielding
of precedence in doorways and conversations. I
am not sure that men do not sometimes offer
their chairs to other men, even where there is
no acknowledged inequality. I note this fact
because it suggests that courtesy *might* similarly
be extended to women even after their attainment
of equal rights. But such a code cannot be
reconciled with the philosophy of The Conde-

scending Man, and I do not blame him for disregarding it.

Such, then, is the first and most formidable obstacle to the attempt of women to acquire political power. The second obstacle is a product of the attempt itself, less formidable because essentially artificial and accidental. I refer to The Obstructive Woman. When this matter began to be agitated it was natural and proper to ask whether any considerable number of women actually wanted to vote. In other words, it was very generally assumed that a right of this sort should be acknowledged when it was earnestly and persistently and widely *asserted*. What was required first of all was an expression of opinion. It was desirable that those women who did *not* wish to vote should say so, and that they should even organize in order that such a disinclination should be brought to light wherever it existed. In canvassing opinion it is important to count the "noes" as well as the "ayes." But organization and counter-organization has developed a contest in which the natural human desire to win has brought about an unconscious but very significant alteration of motives. The pro-suffrage organizations still represent as they did at the beginning the desire of some women to vote. But the anti-suffrage organizations no longer represent merely their members' disinclination to vote, but a determination that those who *are* so inclined shall not succeed. Their first platform was: "We do not want it"; their present platform is: "They shall not have it." Hence The Obstructive Woman.

"Anti-suffrage" *sounds* like "anti-vivisection," and is therefore misleading. It suggests that suffrage is something like vivisection, which is at least painful and injurious to its victims, and that opposition to it is dictated by a misguided chivalry or sentimentality. So hard is it to believe that any body of persons would expend great effort to no end but that of obstruction. "Association Opposed to Woman Suffrage" sounds like "Society for the Prevention of Cruelty to Animals." A visitor from Mars would not unnaturally suppose that "Woman Suffrage" was some form of disease or social abuse, which tender-hearted and public-spirited persons were resolved to suppress. What would be his surprise to learn that it was a boon, a privilege, eagerly craved by the only persons immediately affected, and opposed by other persons whose will no one is proposing to constrain! It is as though the unmusical should organize for the prevention of concerts among the musical, or the indifferent should announce their opposition to the fulfilment of desire.

That Mrs. Arthur M. Dodge, President of the National Association Opposed to Woman Suffrage, should not want to vote is proper enough, but not especially significant. That Miss Katharine B. Davis, Commissioner of Correction in New York City, and head of a department numbering between six and seven hundred voters, should not be allowed to vote, despite her wish to do so, is highly significant. It is a sharp challenge to existing political usage in the name of the existing political creed. But that Mrs. Arthur M. Dodge should seek to prevent Miss Katharine B. Davis from voting is preposterous. It would be incredible if it were not the familiar fact. It can only be accounted for by supposing that what is essentially obstruction is warmed by the passion for victory and idealized by the sentiment of loyalty. Obstruction has acquired the dignity of a Cause.

The Obstructive Woman is a disquieting social and political phenomenon, and complicates what would otherwise be a comparatively simple issue. I may say at once that I should be wholly opposed to compelling The Obstructive Woman to vote. Fortunately, that is not contemplated. To some, however, it might seem a doubtful policy to permit her to vote. Certainly her will in this matter, her impulse to oppose rather than to promote, her inexplicable preference of a manger when there are other equally good beds to lie on—this does tend to disqualify her. In her present mood she is obviously unsuited to the temper of democratic institutions. I do not despair of her, however. She has acquired valuable political experience, and has demonstrated her possession of political aptitude. She is both able and willing to make her voice heard, and to render her will effective. That she should have devoted these gifts to obstruction rather than construction, to repression rather than liberty, may fairly be regarded as an accident. The very fatuousness of her efforts is a sign of her courage and resolution, of her love of power and of her determination to see a thing through when she has once undertaken it. I believe that she has proved her capacity for citizenship, and that when the present confusion of motives is dispelled, after the struggle is over, she will take her place nobly among the rest. I hope, therefore, that even The Obstructive Woman will not be disfranchised.

It is argued, I know, that The Obstructive Woman is not merely obstructive, that she has her own ideals and conception of good. In particular she regards herself as the protagonist of the family and the domestic virtues, and claims the right to be left to her own "sphere." This solicitude for the family is commendable, but is wasteful of good, righteous feeling. Politics need no more draw women from the nursery than men from the ditch. Since women must bear and rear children, and men must feed and clothe them, women have an equal leisure for citizenship, and at least an equal schooling for it.

Furthermore, the removal of arbitrary restrictions upon the exercise of political power means *freedom and fair play for all ideals.* The only grievance that remains is the uncongenial task of acquiring familiarity with public affairs and the labor of going to the polls; which is, I think, to match an annoyance against an injustice. Furthermore, by their present attitude anti-suffrage women condemn themselves to a task that is equally laborious, and which must be more uncongenial. For it is a task of opposition and repression. It involves all the ordinary agencies of political action, but directs them to the stifling of legitimate aspiration. And unless the whole spirit of our institutions is altered, it is a hopeless task. For the motive which they seek to oppose is that irrepressible motive of liberty and equality which finds in democracy its proper soil and native air.

The Condescending Man and The Obstructive Woman are the two most interesting by-products of this latest political revolution. They are characteristic of the phase of struggle and read-justment. They become innocuous the moment they are seen to be what they are. Meanwhile they exert power because they obscure the simpler issue and muddle the minds of well-meaning per-sons. Their strongest ally is that peculiar nervous irritability which we proudly acknowledge as "the American sense of humor." It is an al-most irresistible impulse to giggle at superficial absurdities and ignore the deeper tragic forces that are working beneath. It testifies to an un-canny instinct for the incongruous and its al-most morbid fascination for us. But though the incongruous be comic, the incongruity of the comic itself—laughter out of place—is not comic. There is nothing more painful, more empty, or more blind. Fortunately the impulse to laugh is inhibited by direct personal relations. It needs to merge and hide itself in the crowd. Hence the realities of this issue are most soberly as well as most clearly presented in the confrontation of the individual with his neighbor. It behooves every one who would judge wisely and fairly to observe them there. One may then transfer to women at large those attitudes of tolerance and respect, and those relations of fellow service and common will, which constitute the only tolerable bond between one adult human being and another.